MYP *by Concept*
2

Language & Literature

Language & Literature

MYP by Concept 2

Zara Kaiserimam

Series editor: Paul Morris

Although every effort has been made to ensure that website addresses are correct at time of going to press, Hodder Education cannot be held responsible for the content of any website mentioned in this book. It is sometimes possible to find a relocated web page by typing in the address of the home page for a website in the URL window of your browser.

Hachette UK's policy is to use papers that are natural, renewable and recyclable products and made from wood grown in well-managed forests and other controlled sources. The logging and manufacturing processes are expected to conform to the environmental regulations of the country of origin.

Orders: please contact Hachette UK Distribution, Hely Hutchinson Centre, Milton Road, Didcot, Oxfordshire, OX11 7HH. Telephone: +44 (0)1235 827827. Email education@hachette.co.uk Lines are open from 9 a.m. to 5 p.m., Monday to Friday. You can also order through our website: www.hoddereducation.com

© Zara Kaiserimam 2018
Published by Hodder Education
An Hachette UK Company
Carmelite House, 50 Victoria Embankment, London EC4Y 0DZ

The authorised representative in the EEA is Hachette Ireland, 8 Castlecourt Centre, Dublin 15, D15 XTP3, Ireland (email: info@hbgi.ie)

Impression number   9
Year   2025

All rights reserved. Apart from any use permitted under UK copyright law, no part of this publication may be reproduced or transmitted in any form or by any means, electronic or mechanical, including photocopying and recording, or held within any information storage and retrieval system, without permission in writing from the publisher or under licence from the Copyright Licensing Agency Limited. Further details of such licences (for reprographic reproduction) may be obtained from the Copyright Licensing Agency Limited, www.cla.co.uk.

Cover photo © Consuelo Barreto/123RF.com
Illustrations by DC Graphic Design Limited
Typeset in Frutiger LT Std 45 Light 11/15pt by DC Graphic Design Limited, Hextable, Kent
Printed and bound by CPI Group (UK) Ltd, Croydon, CR0 4YY

A catalogue record for this title is available from the British Library

ISBN 9781471880797

Contents

1 How can we separate fact from fiction? 2

2 What makes a life worth writing about? 32

3 Why do we need to belong? 56

4 Should we forgive and forget? 78

5 Friends forever? 102

6 Do girls run the world? 118

Glossary 150

Acknowledgements 152

How to use this book

Welcome to Hodder Education's *MYP by Concept* Series! Each chapter is designed to lead you through an *inquiry* into the concepts of Language and Literature, and how they interact in real-life global contexts.

Each chapter is framed with a *Key concept* and a *Related concept* and is set in a *Global context*.

The *Statement of Inquiry* provides the framework for this inquiry, and the *Inquiry questions* then lead us through the exploration as they are developed through each chapter.

KEY WORDS

Key words are included to give you access to vocabulary for the topic. **Glossary terms** are highlighted and, where applicable, **search terms** are given to encourage independent learning and research skills.

As you explore, activities suggest ways to learn through *action*.

■ ATL

Activities are designed to develop your *Approaches to Learning* (ATL) skills.

ⓘ Definitions are included for important terms and information boxes are included to give background information, more detail and explanation.

◆ Assessment opportunities in this chapter:

Some activities are *formative* as they allow you to practise certain of the MYP Language and Literature *Assessment Objectives*. Other activities can be used by you or your teachers to assess your achievement against all parts of an Assessment Objective.

Key *Approaches to Learning* skills for MYP Language and Literature are highlighted whenever we encounter them.

Hint

In some of the Activities, we provide Hints to help you work on the assignment. This also introduces you to the new Hint feature in the e-assessment.

EXTENSION

Extension activities allow you to explore a topic further.

Finally, at the end of the chapter you are asked to reflect on what you have learned with our *Reflection table*, maybe to think of new questions brought to light by your learning.

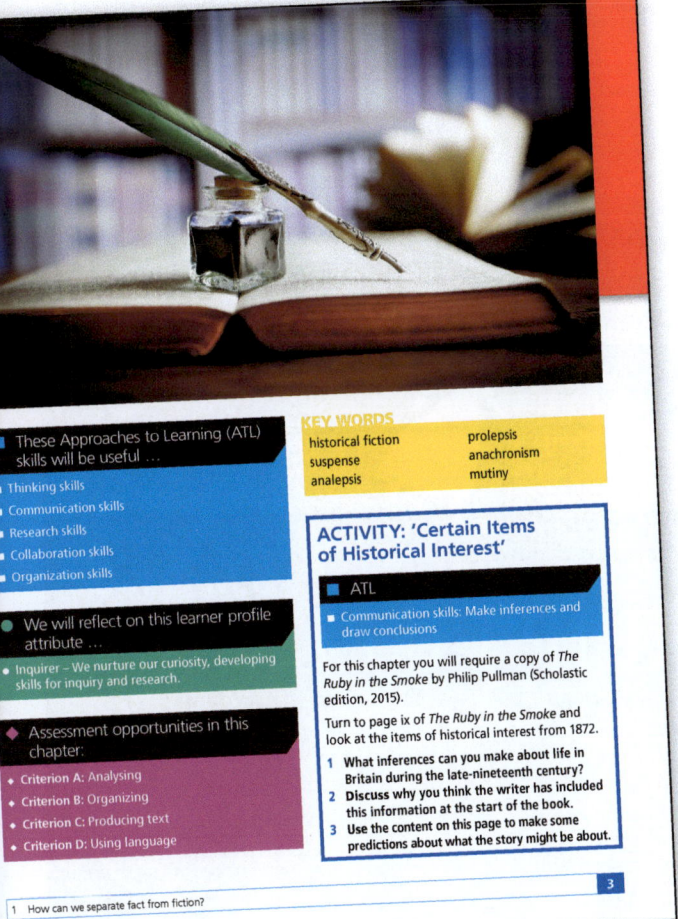

Use this table to reflect on your own learning in this chapter.						
Questions we asked	Answers we found	Any further questions now?				
Factual:						
Conceptual:						
Debatable:						
Approaches to learning you used in this chapter:	Description – what new skills did you learn?	How well did you master the skills?				
		Novice	Learner	Practitioner	Expert	
Collaboration skills						
Communication skills						
Creative-thinking skills						
Information literacy skills						
Media literacy skills						
Reflection skills						
Learner profile attribute(s)	Reflect on the importance of being knowledgeable for your learning in this chapter.					
Knowledgeable						

We have incorporated Visible Thinking – ideas, framework, protocol and thinking routines – from Project Zero at the Harvard Graduate School of Education into many of our activities.

▼ Links to:

Like any other subject, Language and Literature is just one part of our bigger picture of the world. Links to other subjects are discussed.

● We will reflect on this learner profile attribute …

- Each chapter has an *IB learner profile* attribute as its theme, and you are encouraged to reflect on these too.

! Take action

! While the book provides many opportunities for action and plenty of content to enrich the conceptual relationships, you must be an active part of this process. Guidance is given to help you with your own research, including how to carry out research, how to form your own research questions, and how to link and develop your study of Language and Literature to the global issues in our twenty-first-century world.

You are prompted to consider your conceptual understanding in a variety of activities throughout each chapter.

Creativity | Genre; Setting; Point of View | Orientation in Space and Time

1 How can we separate fact from fiction?

○ Writers of the **genre of historical fiction** can shed light on our **orientation in space and time** by using **setting creatively** to help us better understand and learn from the events which have shaped history.

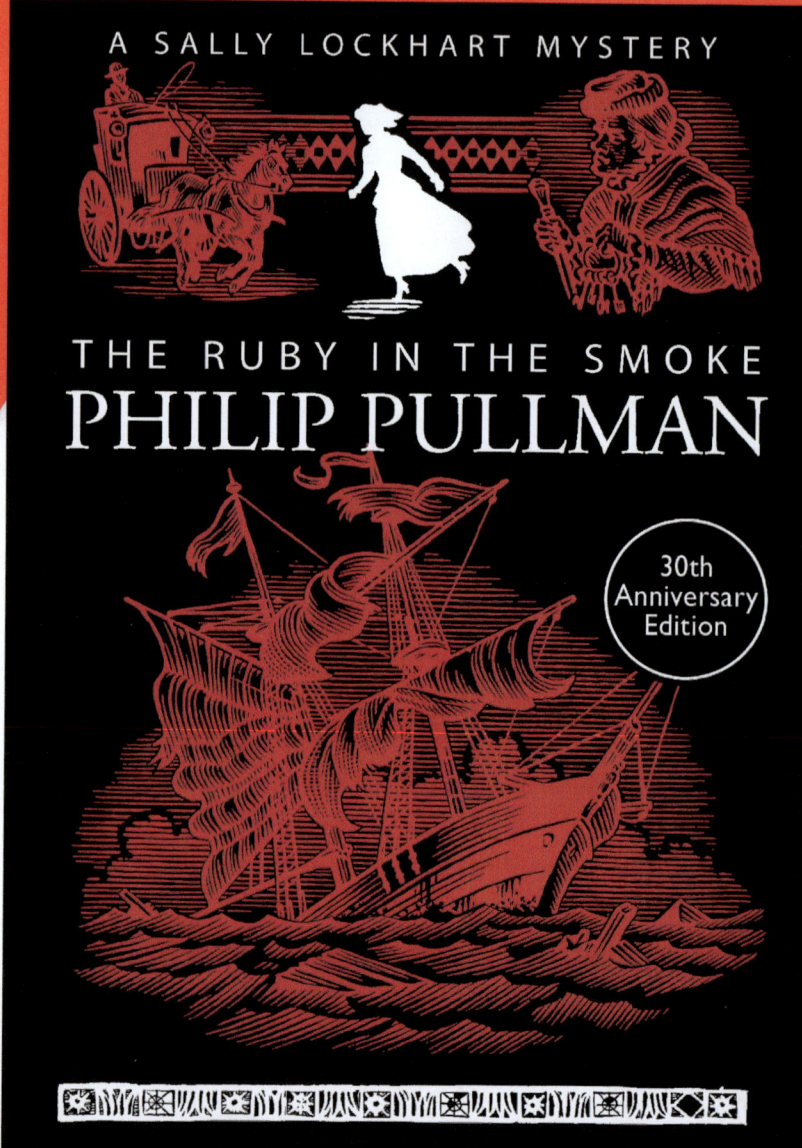

CONSIDER THESE QUESTIONS:

Factual: What is historical fiction? What are the conventions of historical fiction? What was life like in Victorian London?

Conceptual: How can we use fact to create fiction? How can reading historical fiction give us a better understanding of history? What lessons can we learn from reading historical fiction?

Debatable: Does historical fiction blur the boundaries between fiction and reality? Are there enough female protagonists in young adult literature? Is child poverty really a thing of the past?

Now **share and compare** your thoughts and ideas with your partner, or with the whole class.

○ IN THIS CHAPTER, WE WILL ...
- **Find out** what the conventions of historical fiction are.
- **Explore** how historical fiction can give us a better understanding of the past and what lessons we can learn from history.
- **Take action** to raise awareness about issues such as drug addiction and child poverty.

■ These Approaches to Learning (ATL) skills will be useful …

- Thinking skills
- Communication skills
- Research skills
- Collaboration skills
- Organization skills

● We will reflect on this learner profile attribute …

- Inquirer – We nurture our curiosity, developing skills for inquiry and research.

◆ Assessment opportunities in this chapter:

- Criterion A: Analysing
- Criterion B: Organizing
- Criterion C: Producing text
- Criterion D: Using language

KEY WORDS

historical fiction   prolepsis
suspense   anachronism
analepsis   mutiny

ACTIVITY: 'Certain Items of Historical Interest'

■ ATL

- Communication skills: Make inferences and draw conclusions

For this chapter you will require a copy of *The Ruby in the Smoke* by Philip Pullman (Scholastic edition, 2015).

Turn to page ix of *The Ruby in the Smoke* and look at the items of historical interest from 1872.

1. What inferences can you make about life in Britain during the late-nineteenth century?
2. **Discuss** why you think the writer has included this information at the start of the book.
3. **Use** the content on this page to make some predictions about what the story might be about.

1 How can we separate fact from fiction? 3

What is historical fiction?

WHAT IS THE PURPOSE OF HISTORICAL FICTION?

Historical fiction is a **genre** of literature in which the plot of a novel, short story, poem or play is set in the historical past. Historical fiction has existed in its various forms for centuries, but it gained popularity and evolved into the genre as we know it today in the nineteenth century through the work of writers such as Sir Walter Scott, Honoré de Balzac and James Fenimore Cooper.

Today, the genre is as popular as ever (just search for **historical fiction** online and you'll see!) and our reasons for reading historical fiction are as varied as the reasons writers have for creating it. Not only does historical fiction educate us about the past, it allows us to reflect on our own position in history and can help us think about how we live now. It can be an escape as it allows us, both as readers and writers, to imagine other worlds in other times and even gives us an opportunity to temporarily assume other identities. Historical fiction can be used as a safe vehicle through which we can critique our own societies. Walter Scott did precisely that; the situations he presented would have been familiar enough to his audiences, but also different enough to keep himself out of trouble with those he was criticizing!

In this chapter we will further explore the genre of historical fiction by looking closely at an example: *The Ruby in the Smoke*, the first novel in the *Sally Lockhart Quartet* by Philip Pullman. The other books in the series are *The Shadow in the North*, *The Tiger in the Well* and *The Tin Princess*.

ACTIVITY: Five minutes with Philip Pullman

■ **ATL**

- Critical-thinking skills: Evaluate evidence or arguments

Philip Pullman is a prizewinning British author best known for the *His Dark Materials* fantasy trilogy, the first novel of which was adapted as a film under the title *The Golden Compass*.

Follow the link and watch the short video. Complete the tasks which follow:

https://bbc.in/3nWfy73 https://youtu.be/Yd2TNXC4rxU

1 Pullman describes himself as an 'omnivorous' reader. **Interpret** what he means.
2 **Evaluate** the points he makes about the importance of storytelling.
3 **Discuss** what Pullman identifies as the differences between storytellers and writers. How far do you agree with this? **Justify** your ideas.
4 What influence have Pullman's past experiences had on his writing?
5 Do you agree with his view that 'every kind of work has a moral voice'? **Explain** why or why not.

◆ Assessment opportunities

◆ In this activity you have practised skills that are assessed using Criterion A: Analysing.

What are the conventions of historical fiction?

HOW CAN WE USE FACT TO CREATE FICTION?

How does the process of writing historical fiction differ from that of other genres? Do historical fiction novels contain the same elements of writing as other stories? What conventions are unique to fiction of this kind? Can historical novels contain aspects of other genres? Let's find out!

First things first – what makes a historical novel, historical? Well, according to the Historical Novel Society, in order for a novel 'to be deemed historical [it] must have been written at least fifty years after the events described, or to have been written by someone who was not alive at the time of those events (who therefore approaches them only by research)'.

What this means for a budding writer of historical fiction is that research is everything. Establishing a believable historical setting which allows your reader to immerse themselves in the period you have chosen is an incredibly important part of the writing process and in order to achieve this, a writer must ensure that the details they include are accurate – from what the local environment looks like to the very clothes your characters wear or the food they eat.

> How do we know that this character belongs to a bygone era? Use an online dictionary to find out what these objects are.

Her profuse hair, of a colour betwixt brown and flaxen, was arranged in a fanciful and graceful manner in numerous ringlets, to form which art had probably aided nature. These locks were braided with gems, and, being worn at full length, intimated the noble birth and free-born condition of the maiden. A golden chain, to which was attached a small reliquary of the same metal, hung round her neck. She wore bracelets on her arms, which were bare. Her dress was an under-gown and kirtle of pale sea-green silk, over which hung a long loose robe, which reached to the ground, having very wide sleeves, which came down, however, very little below the elbow. This robe was crimson, and manufactured out of the very finest wool. A veil of silk, interwoven with gold, was attached to the upper part of it, which could be, at the wearer's pleasure, either drawn over the face and bosom after the Spanish fashion, or disposed as a sort of drapery round the shoulders.

Ivanhoe by Sir Walter Scott

> Do we learn anything about her social status from these details?

ACTIVITY: What are the conventions of historical fiction?

■ ATL

- Communication skills: Read critically and for comprehension
- Critical-thinking skills: Draw reasonable conclusions and generalizations

In pairs or groups of three, discuss the following:

1. What are the essential components of a story?
2. What differentiates a good story from a bad one?
3. How do works of historical fiction differ from other types of stories? What additional features might they contain?

Now, on your own, read the extracts on pages 5 and 6 and use questions to help you **identify** the conventions of historical fiction.

◆ Assessment opportunities

- In this activity you have practised skills that are assessed using Criterion A: Analysing.

> Consider the clothes she wears and her immediate environment. When and where do you think this extract is set?

---

1 How can we separate fact from fiction?

Battle plans on paper were rare. In fact Bissen had never even seen one. He took the map from Bhan and peered at it more closely. Their position for the start of the battle was clearly marked. They would begin to the right of the British First Army, under the direction of James Willocks, commander of the Indian Corps.

He looked at the position of the German trenches. They seemed so close, the first line sitting right in front of the village.

'Are we to take the village?' he asked Bhan Singh.

His friend nodded.

'And there will be a surprise for our enemies', he whispered.

'What surprise?' asked an excited Jiwan.

Bhan shook his head. 'I cannot say,' he replied as three large rats slid across Bissen's boots and into the water at the base of the trench.

Bissen kicked out and caught rodent flesh. A shriek pierced the air. 'Damn rats!' he said. 'It's a wonder they don't try to eat us as we sleep.'

'Sleep?' asked Bhan Singh. 'I wish I could remember what that means ... How I long for the village of my birth. Instead here I am fighting a white man's war.'

City of Ghosts by Bali Rai

Identify details in the extract which suggest it is set in the historical past. Use these details to make inferences about when and where the extract is set.

What can we learn about the past from the text?

At last her shot being expended, the child stood still and gazed at Hester, with that laughing image of a fiend peeping out – or, whether it peeped out or no, her mother so imagined it – from the unsearchable abyss of her black eyes.

'Child, what art thou?' cried the mother.

'Oh, I am your little Pearl!' answered the child.

But while she said it, Pearl laughed, and began to dance up and down with the humoursome gesticulation of a little imp, whose next freak might be to fly up the chimney.

'Art thou my child, in very truth?' asked Hester.

The Scarlet Letter, Nathaniel Hawthorne

The novel was published in 1850 but is set in seventeenth-century New England. How does the dialogue reveal that the novel is set in the past? Which words in particular suggest this?

In your opinion how important is it to make the **dialogue** in an historical novel sound authentic? How easy would you find it to read a novel which relies heavily on archaic language? Is it completely necessary? **Discuss** with a partner.

ACTIVITY: Historical fiction – top tips

ATL

- Communication skills: Write for different purposes

Author Tanya Landman holding a copy of her book, *The Goldsmith's Daughter*, a novel set in the Aztec empire during the Spanish invasion.

Tanya Landman is the author of several historical fiction novels for young adults. Read the text over the page and **discuss** her top tips for writing historical fiction. Complete the following tasks:

Part 1

1. In your opinion, what is the most valuable piece of advice? **Justify** your response.
2. **Identify** what effect a good work of historical fiction should have on the reader.
3. What important point does Landman make about research?

Part 2

Now, on your own, **synthesize** what you have read and what you have learned in this chapter so far about historical fiction and **create** a guide to writing historical fiction.

You can record/present your ideas any way you like as long as it is an effective tool which can be used by yourself or others.

◆ Assessment opportunities

- In this activity you have practised skills that are assessed using Criterion B: Organizing, Criterion C: Producing text and Criterion D: Using language.

1 How can we separate fact from fiction?

Tanya Landman's top tips for writing historical fiction

The Carnegie-shortlisted author of Apache *and* Buffalo Soldier, *a new book about a young African-American slave after the American Civil War, shares her top tips on making the past come alive in fiction writing.*

My fascination with history started when I was about seven years old and discovered *Stig of the Dump*. Strictly speaking it's not a 'historical novel', but as anyone who's ever read it (and if you haven't read it go away and do so now!) will remember there are the magical chapters when – on Midsummer night – the modern world melts away and Barney finds himself in the Stone Age.

It's a book for younger readers than my historical novels but its author, Clive King, teaches a valuable lesson in how to make the past become the present: you can see the people, taste their food, hear their music, feel the ground shake as a standing stone is moved up the hill.

Writing historical fiction is all about giving a reader Barney's experience of walking into another time and seeing it live and breathe.

1 **When writing historical fiction, the emphasis should be on the 'fiction'**
You're not writing a text book – the story is the most important element. And like any story, you take a character, you give them a problem and either they overcome it (happy ending!) or it overcomes them (a tragic one).

2 **Doing the research is a large part of the fun**
Pick a period you find absolutely gripping, because the more you find out about it the better. Immerse yourself in detail: what people ate, what they wore, where they worked, how they spent their days. You can't do too much research, so be prepared to become a total geek.

3 **Wear your research lightly**
All that information you've crammed into your head should be like an iceberg – most of which will remain unseen. You might know some gloriously obscure facts, but does your reader have to? Avoid cramming information in just because you want to demonstrate how much you know. A story can be so weighed down with detail that it drowns.

4 **History is always written by the victors, so don't believe everything you read**
Historians argue all the time about how to interpret particular events. Throughout time and history people have said one thing and done another. Kings, queens and politicians have always lied and their motives have been misinterpreted. Try and see the other side of the story. Ask 'what if' all the time. What if this person was lying? What if it didn't happen quite the way they said? What if that person was innocent of the crime he was accused of? The 'what if' is meat and drink to a writer of historical fiction.

5 **Tell your story from the inside out**
You know what happened historically but your characters do not, any more than you know what will happen to you tomorrow or next week or next year. People only ever see some of what occurs, and their view will be partial and prejudiced according to their background and beliefs. So don't try to cover every aspect of a historical event and don't try to explain it objectively. Be biased!

ACTIVITY: Introducing Sally

ATL

- Communication skills: Read critically and for comprehension

- Actress Billie Piper as protagonist Sally Lockhart in the television adaptation of *The Shadow in the North*, the second novel in the quartet.

Read Chapter 1 of *The Shadow in the North*, 'The Seven Blessings', and complete the following tasks:

1. **Identify** what narrative voice is used to tell the story.
2. What is the effect of using this type of narrative voice?
3. How is the character of Sally Lockhart introduced?
4. What do we learn about her as the chapter unfolds?
5. What aspects of her character or appearance reveal to us that she belongs to the time period in which the novel is set?
6. **Analyse** the ways in which the writer creates suspense in the novel.

◆ Assessment opportunities

- In this activity you have practised skills that are assessed using Criterion A: Analysing.

Did you know …

… that 'penny blood' or 'penny dreadful' was the name for cheap booklets sold in the nineteenth century which contained tales of adventure, the supernatural or crime and detection?

The format became popular in the 1830s, possibly due to increasing literacy and improved printing technology. The stories were released in serial form, which meant that they were told in instalments or episodes, issued weekly. Each 'number', as they were called, was 8–16 pages long.

In *The Ruby in the Smoke*, Jim Taylor reads a penny dreadful called *Union Jack*, a publication which didn't actually exist until 1894, which makes it an **anachronism**, something that is mistakenly placed in a time period where it doesn't belong.

You can find out more about penny dreadfuls by visiting the link:

www.bl.uk/romantics-and-victorians/articles/penny-dreadfuls

- Penny dreadfuls were very popular during the Victorian period

1 How can we separate fact from fiction?

Flashing back, flashing forward

The Ruby in the Smoke has an **omniscient** narrator. This type of narrator has access to past, present and future events which is why the novel is full of flashbacks and foreshadowing.

When a narrator flashes back to an event in the past, this is known as **analepsis**. This can be seen in the novel when the narrator recalls events from Sally's past, such as the conversation she has with her father before he leaves on his final voyage.

When a narrator flashes forward to an event which hasn't occurred yet, this is known as **prolepsis**. For example, *'Her name was Sally Lockhart; and within fifteen minutes, she was going to kill a man.'*

Prolepsis is similar to **foreshadowing**, a device which hints at events which are going to take place as the plot unfolds.

ACTIVITY: Meanwhile in the novel: Chapter 2

■ ATL

- Communication skills: Read critically and for comprehension

Read Chapter 2 of *The Shadow in the North* and complete the following tasks:

1 **Create** a brief summary of the events of the chapter.
2 **Interpret** what Sally's behaviour at the inquest reveals about Victorian expectations about women.
3 **Analyse** the metaphor of the spider's web on page 15.
4 Which new characters are we introduced to in this chapter?

◆ Assessment opportunities

- ◆ In this activity you have practised skills that are assessed using Criterion A: Analysing.

ACTIVITY: Time travellers

■ ATL

- Information literacy skills: Access information to be informed and inform others
- Creative-thinking skills: Practise visible thinking strategies

In pairs, **discuss** the following questions:

1 **If you could go back in time, which period in history would you choose to visit and in which part of the world?**
2 **Explain why. What appeals to you about this period?**

Over the course of this chapter you will have the opportunity to write part of a historical fiction story set in a period of your choice.

To prepare, carry out some research about a historical period of your choice and create a moodboard to keep a record of your ideas. A moodboard is a collage made up of images, texts and just about anything you can stick down on a page, used to collate ideas or inspiration about a topic of your choice. They're fun to make and will look great displayed in your classroom.

To get started all you need is a piece of A3 paper or card and some glue.

Happy sticking!

◆ Assessment opportunities

- ◆ In this activity you have practised skills that are assessed using Criterion B: Organizing.

How can reading historical fiction give us a better understanding of history?

WHAT WAS LIFE LIKE IN VICTORIAN LONDON?

■ A late-nineteenth century photograph captures some street urchins; children from poor families who lived in the slums and spent the majority of their time on the streets.

■ An engraving by French artist Gustave Doré from *London, a Pilgrimage* (1869). The book, an account of the deprivation and squalor of Victorian London, was the result of a four-year collaboration between Doré and British journalist Blanchard Jerrold.

Books have always provided us with a gateway to the past; today we have access to books spanning hundreds of years and we can use the details they contain to piece together an image of the past. Through books we can access the ideas, attitudes and anxieties of society at the time when these texts were produced.

For instance, from the novels of Jane Austen we can learn about what it was like to be a woman living in England in the nineteenth century, while from the essays of James Baldwin we can develop an understanding of the racial tensions which plagued American society in the early and mid-twentieth century and from the poems of the First World War we can try and empathise with the soldiers who experienced the horrors of warfare.

In fifty or perhaps even a hundred years from now, what do you think future generations will learn about us from reading literature produced today? What does literature from today's world reveal about our lives?

Although the works of literature mentioned above are 'historical' because they were written in the past, they are *not* the same as some of the examples of historical fiction we are exploring in this chapter.

Historical fiction allows readers (as well as writers) an opportunity to immerse themselves in history and learn about the past in an engaging and more accessible way, and in *The Ruby in the Smoke* Pullman takes us on a journey around Victorian London, the seat of Britain's vast Empire at the time.

1 How can we separate fact from fiction?

Activity: The East End

ATL

- Communication skills: Make inferences and draw conclusions; Organize and depict information logically

A great part of *The Ruby in the Smoke* is set in the East End of London during the nineteenth century. The action in the novel is set 16 years before the notorious Jack the Ripper murders.

Before the murders, the affluent inhabitants of the city residing in the West End were oblivious to the plight of the poor who lived and worked in appalling conditions in East London.

As horrible as they were, the Ripper murders played a role in raising awareness about the deprivation in the East End. What role do you think newspaper coverage of the crimes played in this?

Look at the text below and opposite and complete the following tasks:

1. **Identify** the genre, audience and **purpose** of the text.
2. What are the **connotations** of the word 'teeming'?
3. What was life like during the nineteenth century? **Organize** your response in a paragraph and use evidence from the text to support your answer.
4. **Analyse** the quotation 'the hunting grounds of Jack the Ripper'.
5. **Evaluate** how the writer has made the information:
   a. informative and easier to understand for the readers
   b. more interesting to read for the audience.

Organize your answer for Question 5 using paragraphs and make reference to language, stylistic choices and **presentational devices**.

Headline and layout – Is this text really a newspaper? What is the effect of presenting the text in this way? Use the internet to find out more about newspapers in the nineteenth century.

Pictures and photographs – What do these images depict? Why has the writer included them and how do they relate to the content of the text?

Timeline – How might this make the information more accessible for readers?

LONDON NEWS

No. 1   15 May to 2 November 2008   One Halfpenny

JACK THE RIPPER AND THE EAST END

Between April 1888 and February 1891, eleven women were brutally murdered in London's East End.

The 'Whitechapel murders' were believed to be the work of a serial killer. The blood-red signature on a letter to the press named him as Jack the Ripper. The story of the Whitechapel murders — acts of unspeakable violence committed in the teeming city — has been endlessly recycled. Familiar today throughout the world, it has assumed the status of urban legend.

THE ELEVEN MURDERED WOMEN

Emma Smith (1843 – 3 April 1888)
Martha Tabram (1849 – 7 August 1888)
Mary Ann Nichols (1845 – 31 August 1888)
Annie Chapman (1841 – 8 September 1888)
Elizabeth Stride (1843 – 30 September 1888)
Catherine Eddowes (1842 – 30 September 1888)
Mary Jane Kelly (c.1863 – 9 November 1888)
Rose Mylett (1862 – 20 December 1888)
Alice McKenzie (c.1849 – 17 July 1889)
Torso of an unknown woman (found 10 September 1889)
Frances Coles (1865 – 13 February 1891)

Did you know…

… that the Indian writer and reformer Behramji Malabari was horrified by the *'millions, ill-fed and housed in miserable hovels'* he encountered on his trip to London in the 1890s? Malabari recorded his account of English life in his travelogue, *The Indian Eye on English Life, or Rambles of a pilgrim reformer.*

The views he expressed about what he saw in the East End echoed those held by the British about life in India at the time. Malabari's illuminating account reveals that despite the Empire's wealth and power, a large proportion of British society lived in debilitating poverty.

East End mother and children, c.1900

East End blind street musicians, c.1900

Outside an East End music hall, c.1872

THE EAST END IN 1888

Over a million inhabitants crowded the streets and alleys of the East End. It was seen as a world apart – a place of poverty, filth, crime and degradation – which outsiders entered at their peril. Just a few streets away from the wealth of the City of London, the poor of Whitechapel and Spitalfields struggled to survive. A maze of dark, overcrowded courts and passages became the hunting grounds of Jack the Ripper.

The East End provided plentiful cheap labour. Immigrants crowded into the area hoping to find casual work or unskilled labouring jobs. Some were forced to enter the workhouse. Many found work in the docks, where competition for jobs was fierce and conditions were harsh. Others toiled in 'sweated' tailoring and boot-making workshops or worked at home making brushes or skinning rabbits.

HOUSING

The women murdered by Jack the Ripper were typical of the thousands who slept in the East End's common lodging houses. For four pence, these often filthy places provided a bed for the night in a dormitory, and access to a common kitchen. As more and more people crowded into the East End, properties were constantly sub-let. Whole families or groups of strangers – often a dozen people – crammed together in a single small room to cook, eat and sleep, sharing beds or sleeping on the floor.

DRINK

The women murdered by Jack the Ripper were addicted to alcohol. In a world of extreme deprivation where there was little hope, drink offered a form of comfort and escape. Whitechapel and Spitalfields were crowded with pubs and 'gin palaces': one mile-long section of Whitechapel Road boasted over 45 of them.

Look out for this symbol throughout the exhibition. It will lead you to some of the key information available at the time of the murders. Analyse the evidence first-hand and leave your conclusions on the board at the end of the exhibition.

Subheadings – Why has the writer chosen to organize the text using subheadings?

◆ Assessment opportunities

- In this activity you have practised skills that are assessed using Criterion A: Analysing, Criterion B: Organizing and Criterion D: Using language.

1 How can we separate fact from fiction?

ACTIVITY: 'a rich and fruitful land' – The great divide

ATL

- Communication skills: Read critically and for comprehension
- Critical-thinking skills: Recognize unstated assumptions and bias

■ In his collection of poems, *Songs of Innocence and of Experience*, William Blake questions and criticizes the practices of his society.

■ Blake produced the illustrations for his own books

William Blake was an English Romantic poet and painter. During the late-eighteenth century, when Blake was writing, industrialization and imperial enterprise meant that Britain was one of the most powerful countries in the world. Despite this, there was a great disparity between the rich and the poor.

In his poetry, Blake challenged the way Britain perceived itself as a super-power and highlighted the injustices of a system that served only the needs of the rich and powerful.

Read the poem below and complete the questions which follow:

1. What can you infer about how Britain perceived itself during the late-eighteenth century?
2. Does Blake share this view of Britain? **Justify** your answer using evidence from the text.
3. **Identify** which sentence moods appear in the poem. Choose an example which conveys Blake's ideas and attitudes and **analyse** the effect.
4. **Identify** and **analyse** examples of language Blake uses to evoke sympathy for the children of London in the poem.
5. **Interpret** the message of the last two stanzas and explain the effect of the use of nature imagery.

◆ Assessment opportunities

♦ In this activity you have practised skills that are assessed using Criterion A: Analysing.

Holy Thursday: Songs of Experience

Is this a holy thing to see,
In a rich and fruitful land,
Babes reduc'd to misery,
Fed with cold and usurous hand?

Is that trembling cry a song?
Can it be a song of joy?
And so many children poor?
It is a land of poverty!

And their sun does never shine.
And their fields are bleak & bare.
And their ways are fill'd with thorns.
It is eternal winter there.

For where'er the sun does shine,
And where'er the rain does fall:
Babe can never hunger there,
Nor poverty the mind appall.

William Blake

Language & Literature for the IB MYP 2: by Concept

How to tackle a close reading task

A **close reading** of a passage can help you develop a precise interpretation of a text and help you gain a deeper understanding of a writer's craft. Being able to look closely at a text is an essential skill for all Language and Literature students.

Follow the guidelines below to help you tackle close reading tasks with ease.

Active reading

1. Read the text carefully to ensure you have a general understanding of it.

2. Read actively! Make sure you have a pencil in your hand to jot down what you feel are the key points of the text. Consider the message, themes and **context**.

3. Read the text again and this time annotate it in detail. Highlight key quotations. Focus on language used to convey meaning and any literary devices. Do you notice any patterns? Are certain words or types of words repeated? What is the writer trying to achieve?

4. Plan your response.

Planning

You have a limited amount of time and words so you must be selective. Don't attempt to write about everything. Just focus on a few key quotations.

1. Select your quotations. Make sure they are long enough and contain significant language and literary features which will allow you to carry out *meaningful* analysis.

2. Decide how you are going to tackle the text. Try to do this logically. You can either approach the text 'chronologically' (start at the beginning and work through the rest of the text in order) or 'thematically'.

3. Write a brief plan to help keep you focused while you write.

Writing

1. At the start *briefly* contextualize the text (what is it about?). You should spend no more than a line or two on this.

2. Choose your first quotation and use PEA paragraphs to organize your writing. For help with how to structure a PEA paragraph refer back to *Language and Literature Book 1*, page 69.

3. Try to make your paragraphs cohesive. Think carefully about how you will move from one paragraph to the next.

■ **Close reading can help you develop a deeper understanding of a text**

1 How can we separate fact from fiction?

Links to: Individuals and Societies/Geography

A wide gap between the rich and the poor still exists in many countries around the world today.

Using the internet, carry out some research about the places in the world where there is the widest gap between the richest and the poorest people who live there.

Find out about:

1 The causes of this economic inequality.
2 The consequences of this inequality.
3 How places where there isn't such a big gap between the rich and the poor manage to achieve greater economic equality. In pairs, discuss what could be learned from them.

ACTIVITY: Setting the scene – part 1

ATL

- Communication skills: Read critically and for comprehension

In Chapter 2, read the section which starts 'Beyond the Tower of London…' and ends '… with a rope stretched across the middle.' Then answer the questions below.

1 **Identify** any conventions of historical fiction in the passage.
2 **Infer** why the writer has included this passage. What purpose does it serve? What message or ideas is the writer trying to convey?
3 **Compare and contrast** Pullman's description of the East End with the one provided in the museum guide you looked at earlier in this chapter.
4 **Evaluate** how effectively the writer has established setting. **Justify** your response using examples of language and stylistic choices made by Pullman.
5 **Select** one key quotation from the text, **analyse** it and write a PEA paragraph about how Pullman has established setting in the novel.

◆ Assessment opportunities

- In this activity you have practised skills that are assessed using Criterion A: Analysing.

ACTIVITY: Setting the scene – part 2 – time to craft

■ **ATL**

- Creative-thinking skills: Create original works and ideas

Look back at your moodboard and at the research you carried out about your chosen historical period.

Use the information you have gathered to write a description which conveys the setting of your story. Aim to write at least 200 words and use a word processor.

Stuck? You can use Pullman's example from the previous task to help you, and you should think carefully about your use of language and supporting details.

Are your descriptive writing skills a little rusty? Follow the link for a quick refresher: www.youtube.com/watch?v=pcuAW31gsXs

Once you have finished your piece, share your work with the whole class. You could use an online sharing platform, such as Padlet, https://padlet.com. Ask your teacher to set up a page where you can all post your writing.

Read and evaluate your peers' writing and make sure you leave both positive and constructive feedback by typing in the comments section of each post.

◆ Assessment opportunities

- In this activity you have practised skills that are assessed using Criterion C: Producing text and Criterion D: Using language.

ACTIVITY: Meanwhile in the novel: Chapter 3

■ **ATL**

- Communication skills: Read critically and for comprehension

Read Chapter 3 of *The Ruby in the Smoke* and complete the tasks:

1. What do you think the significance of Sally's nightmares might be?
2. What elements from other literary genres can you **identify** in the chapter?
3. How is a sense of fear conveyed in Chapter 3?
4. The novel is made up of multiple texts; in addition to the main third person omniscient narrative, we have written accounts, letters, newspaper clippings, telegrams and advertisements. In pairs **discuss** what the effect of this is.

◆ Assessment opportunities

- In this activity you have practised skills that are assessed using Criterion A: Analysing.

DOES HISTORICAL FICTION BLUR THE BOUNDARIES BETWEEN FICTION AND REALITY?

Stories like *The Ruby in the Smoke* blend together history and fiction. Real events are fused with those imagined by the author and it is not uncommon to find actual historical figures alongside invented characters.

Pat Barker's *Regeneration* is one example where the fictional elements are so seamlessly interwoven with the real, that it can be difficult to decipher where the story ends and where history begins. In Barker's novel, the stories of imagined characters such as Billy Prior and David Burns are used to shed light on the experiences of many soldiers during the First World War, while the details about real historical figures (Siegfried Sassoon and Wilfred Owen) give the text a sense of authenticity.

As readers of historical fiction we must be able to exercise our critical-thinking skills and learn how to separate fiction from reality when exploring works of the genre.

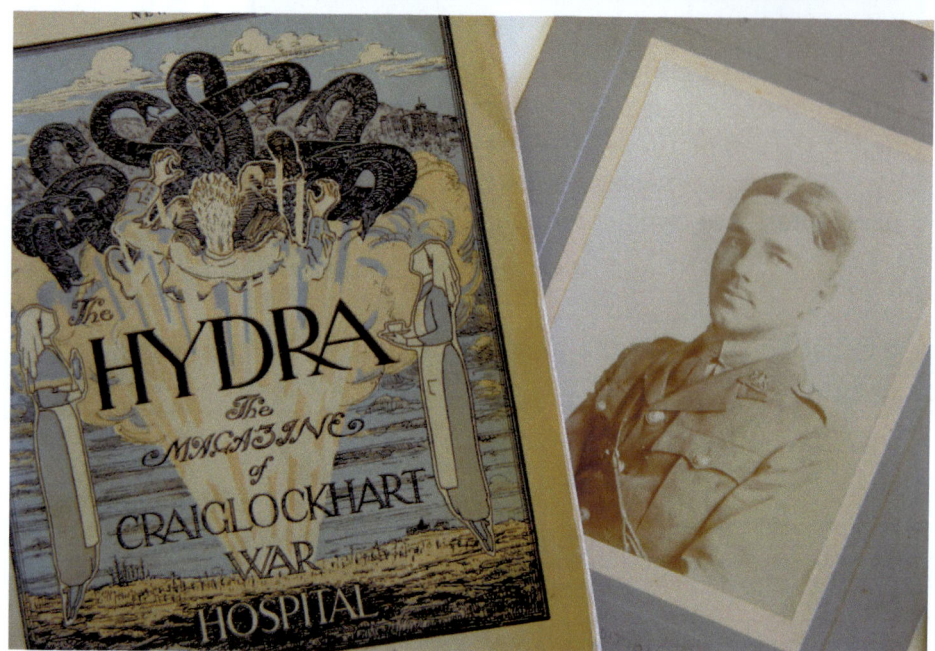

■ Soldier poets of the First World War, Wilfred Owen and Siegfried Sassoon, are resurrected in *Regeneration* by historical fiction writer Pat Barker.

ACTIVITY: Fact check – separating fact from the fiction

■ ATL

- Information literacy skills: Access information to be informed and inform others

Can you separate the facts from the fiction? Copy and complete the table below and use the first column to list any 'historical' details that are mentioned in *The Ruby in the Smoke* Chapter 4, 'The Mutiny'; these could be events, places, objects or people, so look out for proper nouns. You can add as many rows as you need.

Once you have completed the table, use a search engine to find out which details in your list are 'fact' and which are 'fiction'. Make some notes about what you learn in the relevant column.

Next, compile a list of key quotations relating to each item.

'Historical' details	Fact or fiction?	What did you find out?	Key quotations from the novel

◆ Assessment opportunities

- In this activity you have practised skills that are assessed using Criterion B: Organizing.

So far in this chapter we have learned about the conventions of the genre of historical fiction through exploring various literary examples. In addition, we have developed a better understanding of some of the historical contexts referred to in Pullman's novel, *The Ruby in the Smoke*.

▼ Links to: Individuals and Societies/ History

The Indian Mutiny

Look at the painting below by Edward Armitage. In pairs, discuss your initial impressions of the painting. Use the questions below to guide your discussion and make sure you can justify your responses with reference to the image.

- What message do you think the writer is trying to convey?
- What feelings might it evoke in viewers of the painting?
- What do you think the tiger in the picture represents? Who is the woman in the painting?

■ *Retribution*, 1858

Use a search engine to find out the answers to the questions and discuss how you feel about the painting now.

Armitage's painting was completed in 1858, a year after the Indian Mutiny, an event which is alluded to in *The Ruby in the Smoke*. The mutiny provides a historical backdrop to the events that haunt Sally throughout the novel.

In pairs **discuss** the language used by Major Marchbanks in his narrative in Chapter 4 and make some inferences about the Mutiny.

'the terrible storm which was to break over us in the Mutiny'

'horrors and savagery'

'deeds of heroism shining like beacons amid scenes of hideous carnage'

You can find out more about the **Indian Mutiny of 1857** by visiting:

https://bbc.in/2Kvh4Pl.

1 How can we separate fact from fiction?

Are there enough female protagonists in young adult literature?

WHAT CAN WE LEARN ABOUT THE ROLE OF WOMEN IN SOCIETY DURING THE NINETEENTH CENTURY?

When we look back at history, we find that some voices are less prominent than others; the voices of people from minority groups and women are often drowned out by the voices of men or those in power. Historical fiction allows us as writers to address this issue and enables us to offer readers a retelling of history from an alternative point of view.

Pullman's decision to use a female protagonist gives us a different **perspective** on life in Victorian London and through Sally's experiences, behaviour and interactions with others, we get a good sense of what life would have been like for women in society at that time.

Although Sally, Rosa and even the wicked Mrs Holland are all strong, independent-minded women, in 1872, the year in which the novel is set, opportunities for women in terms of work and education would have been limited. However, things were beginning to change; it was in 1870 that the Married Women's Property Act was introduced, and this allowed women rights over their own property or earnings; before this, everything belonged to their husbands.

How much do you know about the history of women's rights in your own country? Have things changed for women in society since the nineteenth century? Discuss these questions with a partner.

ACTIVITY: Women in Victorian England

■ ATL

- Communication skills: Make inferences and draw conclusions

'And what I do know is so ... I don't know how to put it. It's just not the sort of things that girls know.'

Sally, Chapter 11

In pairs, **discuss** Sally's quotation and see if you can create a list of 'the sort of things that girls know'.

Do you think Victorian ideas about what girls knew, or should know, differ from ideas about what girls know in our world today?

Read the nineteenth-century texts opposite and complete these tasks.

1. Are these texts written by men or women? Explain why you think this.
2. **Interpret** the message the writer intends to convey about women in each text. Which writer's ideas or attitudes about women do you prefer? Explain why.
3. **Identify** and **analyse** the language used by the writers to express their ideas and attitudes.
4. **Compare and contrast** the texts. What do they reveal about changing attitudes towards women in society?
5. How do the characters of Sally and Rosa challenge existing Victorian stereotypes about women?
6. Paying particular attention to what you learn in Chapters 7 and 8, but making reference to the rest of the novel, **create** a detailed IB learner profile for Sally. What learner profile characteristics does she possess? Which does she lack? For each characteristic write a brief explanation and provide a quotation from the text to **justify** your ideas.

◆ Assessment opportunities

- In this activity you have practised skills that are assessed using Criterion A: Analysing, Criterion B: Organizing and Criterion D: Using language.

- Towards the end of the Victorian era, women's roles were changing; however educated, working women were a cause of great anxiety as it was believed that they threatened the institution of marriage and traditional family values.

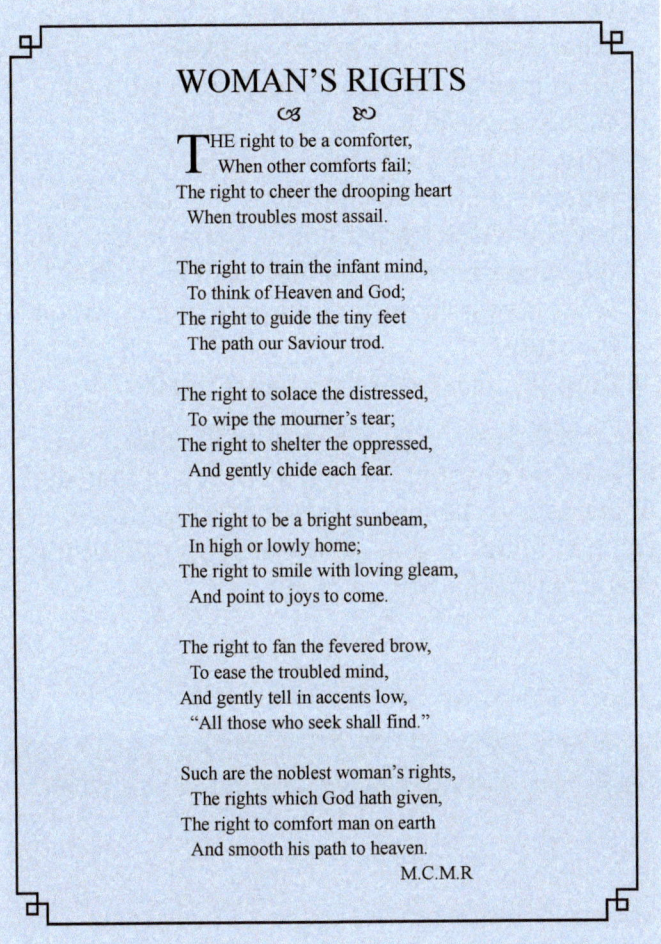

Teach young women from their childhood upwards that marriage is their single career, and it is inevitable that they should look upon every hour which is not spent in promoting this sublime end and aim as so much subtracted from life. Penetrated with unwholesome excitement in one part of their existence, they are penetrated with killing ennui in the next. If mothers would only add to their account of marriage as the end of a woman's existence – which may be right or it may not – a definition of marriage as an association with a reasonable and reflective being, they would speedily effect a revolution in the present miserable system. As it is, the universe to her is only a collection of rich bachelors in search of wives, and of odious rivals who are contending with her for one or more of these two wary prizes. She thinks of nothing except her private affairs. She is indifferent to politics, to literature – in a word, to anything that requires thought. She reads novels of a kind, because novels are all about Love, and love had once something to do with marriage, her own peculiar and absorbing business. Beyond this her mind does not stir.

Saturday Review, 1887

1 How can we separate fact from fiction?

ACTIVITY: Writing character

ATL

- Organization skills: Set goals that are challenging and realistic
- Creative-thinking skills: Create original works and ideas

Part 1

The *Invisible College* is a series of lessons in creative writing which draws on archived recordings of famous writers talking about the craft.

Follow the link below and listen to the **BBC podcast, *Lesson Four: Creating Characters*.**

https://bbc.in/2Nl724S

Copy the table below. As you listen, fill in your table and use what you learn to set yourself some targets for your own writing.

Writer	Words of wisdom	Target
Muriel Spark		
Baroness Orczy		
Graham Greene		
Arthur Machen		

■ *The Scarlet Pimpernel* is the eponymous hero of Baroness Orczy's historical fiction series set during the French Revolution.

Part 2

You've already set the scene for your historical fiction novel so now it's time to bring a character to life.

Take another look at your moodboard and at the research you carried out about your chosen historical period. Do you know enough about what people were like at the time? If not, you might need to do some more research before you start writing.

Use the following questions to help you develop a character. For each one, jot down a couple of ideas.

- Is your character male or female?
- Where does your character live?
- Where is your character from?
- How old is your character?
- What is your character called?
- What does your character look like?
- What kind of childhood/background did your character have?
- Who else is in your character's life?
- What kind of personality does your character have? What IB learner profile characteristics do they possess? Which do they need to develop?
- What is your character's purpose or motivation in the story?
- Does your character have any secrets?

Use the answers to your questions to write a description of your character. In novels, a character develops and changes as the story progresses so you don't have to give away *everything* about the character in your first description.

◆ **Assessment opportunities**

♦ In this activity you have practised skills that are assessed using Criterion C: Producing text and Criterion D: Using language.

Links to: Visual Arts – Photography

In *The Shadow in the North*, Frederick Garland is a photographer who takes great pride in his art. However, Sally soon convinces him to produce and sell stereographic pictures which were very popular with the public at the time.

You can learn more about stereographs by visiting:

www.vam.ac.uk/blog/factory-presents/stereographs

You could have a go at making your own stereographs in your Art or Photography lessons.

ACTIVITY: Where have all the brave girls gone?

ATL

- Collaboration skills: Listen actively to other perspectives and ideas
- Critical-thinking skills: Gather and organize relevant information to formulate an argument

■ Are girls in young adult fiction really defined by their love lives rather than their adventures?

Based on your own experiences of reading young adult literature, do you think that there is a shortage of strong female protagonists?

Take a poll in your class to see how many of you agree or disagree with the following statement:

'In young adult literature, girls are defined by their love lives rather than their adventures.'

What did you find? Were you surprised by the results? Can you list any young adult fiction where the statement applies? Or perhaps you know some examples that you could use to undermine the statement?

Use the statement as a topic for a class debate.

Visit the links below and read the two texts to help you develop your ideas, arguments and counter arguments.

www.theguardian.com/books/booksblog/2013/aug/24/where-have-all-brave-girls-gone-kate-mosse

www.theguardian.com/childrens-books-site/2014/apr/29/where-are-all-the-heroines-teen-fiction

◆ Assessment opportunities

- In this activity you have practised skills that are assessed using Criterion B: Organizing.

1 How can we separate fact from fiction?

WHAT LESSONS CAN WE LEARN FROM READING HISTORICAL FICTION?

In the opening lines of the 1953 novel *The Go Between*, L.P. Hartley's aged narrator states that *'the past is a foreign country: they do things differently there.'* Historical fiction allows us to travel back in time and view historical events from a modern vantage point. Through this lens we can interrogate the past and unravel the bias which can sometimes be found in texts which have been used to document history.

In *The Ruby in the Smoke*, Pullman presents readers with a critique of some of the more negative aspects of Empire through presenting the impact of the opium trade on Bedwell. Pullman also induces empathy for the thousands of city dwellers stricken with poverty, many of them children, by giving us a glimpse into the world of the 'mudlarks'.

In the pages of historical fiction novels, we often encounter characters like Sally who possess views which seem not to belong to their time. This can seem anachronistic, but it is important that we see stories of this genre as more than just history lessons. Historical fiction can be a vehicle through which we can reflect on the past, and learn lessons which can change our perspective about issues in our world today.

HOMELESS !

ACTIVITY: The evils of empire

■ **ATL**

- Communication skills: Read critically and for comprehension
- Critical-thinking skills: Draw reasonable conclusions and generalizations

Read Chapters 9 and 10 of *The Ruby in the Smoke* and complete the following tasks.

1 In pairs, **discuss** what you know about opium. Use the internet to find out about **how opium is used today**.
2 On pages 80 and 81, how does Reverend Bedwell describe opium? **Analyse** the language he uses and comment on the effect. Can you **identify** any stylistic choices?
3 What can you infer about the availability of opium in England at the time the novel is set? How do you feel about this?
4 Based on what you have read so far, what have you learned about the negative effects of opium? How does the use of opium affect Matthew Bedwell? You may want to look back at Chapter 6.
5 In Chapter 10, what do you learn about the role of the British Empire in the increasing use of opium in China? How does Pullman feel about this?

◆ **Assessment opportunities**

- In this activity you have practised skills that are assessed using Criterion A: Analysing.

ACTIVITY: Meanwhile in the novel: Chapters 13–16

■ **ATL**

- Communication skills: Read critically and for comprehension

Read Chapters 13–16 of the novel.

1 **Summarize** what you learn from Matthew Bedwell's narrative.
2 What was Sally's father's dying message? **Interpret** what it means.
3 What does Sally purchase in Chapter 14? What is the **symbolism** of this object?
4 In these chapters, how does Pullman establish an authentic setting?

◆ **Assessment opportunities**

- In this activity you have practised skills that are assessed using Criterion A: Analysing.

1 How can we separate fact from fiction?

ACTIVITY: Multiculturalism in the city

■ ATL

- Information literacy skills: Access information to be informed and inform others

The Ruby in the Smoke is interspersed with references to the growing multicultural community in London's East End in the nineteenth century. The docklands were a first stop for many migrants, including sailors from China, Somalia and Goa, who settled in the East End because of the cheap rents.

Today, London is the one of the most diverse cities in the world; with over 200 languages spoken there daily, it is the most multicultural city in Europe and continues to grow. This cultural diversity has had a largely positive impact on the city.

- How diverse is the city where you are from? Which different communities have made it their home? What positive impact have they had? How long have these communities been a part of your city?
- Carry out a research project to trace the presence of different communities in the city or country you are from and create a presentation for your class.

Alternatively, you could focus on the communities mentioned in the novel.

Here are some links which might be useful:

www.oldbaileyonline.org/static/Chinese.jsp

www.museumoflondon.org.uk/schools/learning-resources

■ J. Salter, *The Asiatic in England: sketches of sixteen years' work among Orientals*

◆ Assessment opportunities

◆ In this activity you have practised skills that are assessed using Criterion B: Organizing.

EXTENSION

Kedgeree!

In Chapter 17, Sally makes 'kedgeree' for her friends. Use the internet to find out about **what kedgeree is and where it originated from**.

Do you know of any foods which are popular in your home country that have exotic origins? Discuss in pairs.

ACTIVITY: Is child poverty really a thing of the past?

Throughout the novel we encounter a number of instances of child poverty. In Victorian England it was not uncommon for poor children to work for their living instead of attending school. The conditions that these children worked in were often dangerous and the wages low.

In Chapter 17, Jim and Adelaide run into Paddy, the leader of a gang of 'mudlarks' – children who scavenged along the river banks during low tide for objects that they may have been able to sell. Read the description from 'The room they entered…' to '…A foul thick smell filled the air.'

Now, in pairs, discuss the following:

1 Is life better and safer for children in Britain today than it was in the nineteenth century? Explain why. What about in other parts of the world?
2 How many children do you think live in poverty in Britain today? What about worldwide? Use the internet to find out.
3 How does this number make you feel? Are you shocked? Surprised? Angry? Sad?

◆ Assessment opportunities

- In this activity you have practised skills that are assessed using Criterion B: Organizing.

ACTIVITY: Meanwhile in the novel: Chapters 18, 19 and 20

■ ATL

- Communication skills: Make inferences and draw conclusions

Read Chapters 18, 19 and 20 and complete the tasks.

1 How is the ruby described on page 185? **Comment on the use of language and stylistic choices.**
2 How does Pullman create a sense of suspense and tension in these chapters?
3 What do you learn from Mrs Holland's narrative? Does Pullman evoke sympathy for her in Chapter 18?
4 What do you learn about Sally's gun in Chapter 19? What does she wish for in relation to her weapon? Can you link this to any earlier examples of foreshadowing in the novel?
5 How does the novel end?

◆ Assessment opportunities

- In this activity you have practised skills that are assessed using Criterion A: Analysing.

1 How can we separate fact from fiction?

> ! **Take action: Opportunity to apply learning through action …**

! **Start a historical fiction society or club:** Reading historical fiction doesn't just improve your understanding of the past; it can help you understand your own world better! Get others reading by meeting regularly to discuss fiction of the genre. Need some inspiration? Follow this link for some ideas:

www.goodreads.com/genres/young-adult-historical-fiction

! **Write, write, write!:** Do you want to find out more about a historical period that has always fascinated you? Write about it! To write a historical novel you'll have to carry out some research. Writing historical fiction will allow you to immerse yourself in the past.

! **Take action about some of the issues raised in the novel:** Angry about the harmful effects of drug addiction? Horrified by the statistics on child poverty? Then do something about it! Raise awareness by creating leaflets and posters; raise funds by organizing charity events in your school or local area. On a more positive note, you might want to celebrate the multiculturalism in your community.

SOME SUMMATIVE PROBLEMS TO TRY

Use these problems to apply and extend your learning in this chapter. These tasks are designed so that you can evaluate your learning using the Language and Literature criteria.

Task 1

- Choose one of the following questions and write an essay-style response.
- Organize your response using PEA paragraphs.
- You must refer to *The Ruby in the Smoke* in your answer.
- Make sure you quote from the text to support your ideas.
- Aim to write at least four PEA paragraphs.

Historical fiction creates different, more inclusive versions of history. To what extent is this true of The Ruby in the Smoke?

Writers of historical fiction are not under the same obligation as historians to find evidence for the statements they make. To what extent is this evident in the writing of Philip Pullman?

Task 2

- Use one of the historical images opposite and over the page as a prompt for writing a novel opening.
- You can spend a lesson carrying out research for your assessment.

■ A tiger hunt, India, nineteenth century

■ Young people listening to a gramophone, Norway, 1930s

1   How can we separate fact from fiction?

■ A wedding in Japan, 1940s

■ *Figures on the Beach*, Pierre Auguste Renoir, France, 1890

■ *Gassed*, John Singer Sargent, 1919

Reflection

In this chapter we have developed an understanding of the conventions of the **genre** of historical fiction through a comprehensive study of Philip Pullman's novel *The Ruby in the Smoke*. In addition we have learned how writers can use **setting creatively** to give us an insightful look at the past. We have seen how historical fiction can shed light on our **orientation in space and time** and how we can learn more about our own world through exploring history. We have also tried our hand at becoming writers of historical fiction.

Use this table to reflect on your own learning in this chapter					
Questions we asked	Answers we found	Any further questions now?			
Factual: What is historical fiction? What are the conventions of historical fiction? What was life like in Victorian London?					
Conceptual: How can we use fact to create fiction? How can reading historical fiction give us a better understanding of history? What lessons can we learn from reading historical fiction?					
Debatable: Does historical fiction blur the boundaries between fiction and reality? Are there enough female protagonists in young adult literature? Is child poverty really a thing of the past?					
Approaches to learning you used in this chapter:	Description – what new skills did you learn?	How well did you master the skills?			
		Novice	Learner	Practitioner	Expert
Thinking skills					
Communication skills					
Research skills					
Collaboration skills					
Organization skills					
Learner profile attribute(s)	Reflect on the importance of inquiry for your learning in this chapter.				
Inquirer					

1 How can we separate fact from fiction?

Communication · Genre; Context · Identities and Relationships

2 What makes a life worth writing about?

The **genre** of biography not only enables us to preserve and **communicate** individual histories as writers, but allows us as readers to develop an understanding of how our social **context** and **relationships** with others can play a key role in shaping our **identities**.

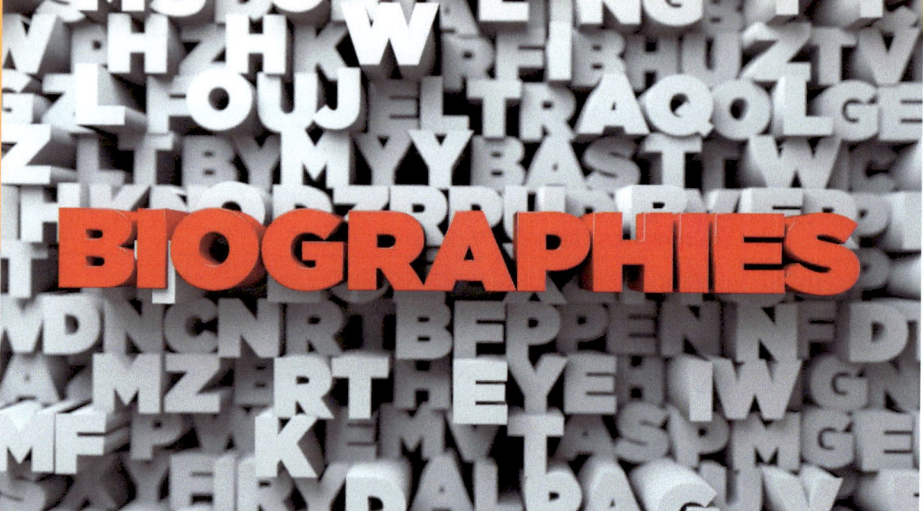

CONSIDER AND ANSWER THESE QUESTIONS:

Factual: What is a biography? What is a biopic?

Conceptual: Why should we read and write biographies?

Debatable: What makes a life worth writing about? Can a writer or artist's biography give us a better understanding of their work?

Now **share and compare** your thoughts and ideas with your partner, or with the whole class.

○ IN THIS CHAPTER, WE WILL …
- **Find out** what biographies are and how to write them.
- **Explore** why we should read and write biographies and what we can learn from them.
- **Take action** to share the stories of ordinary people.

■ These Approaches to Learning (ATL) skills will be useful …
- Thinking skills
- Communication skills
- Creative-thinking skills
- Research skills
- Collaboration skills
- Organization skills

◆ Assessment opportunities in this chapter:
- **Criterion A:** Analysing
- **Criterion B:** Organizing
- **Criterion C:** Producing text
- **Criterion D:** Using language

- We will reflect on this learner profile attribute …
- Inquirer – We nurture our curiosity, developing skills for inquiry and research.

KEY WORDS

biography
biographer
biopic
bibliography
obituary

THINK-PAIR-SHARE

1 On your own, consider the quotation, *'Always live your life with your biography in mind'*. Think about what it means and what you think about the message the writer, Marisha Pessl, is trying to convey.
2 Take a couple of minutes to jot down what you would like people to know about your life and experiences. What are the defining moments of your life so far? Who and/or what matters the most to you?
3 In pairs, discuss the quotation and share what you wrote for task 2.

Although the genre of **biography** writing stretches right back to the days of antiquity, the trend for documenting the lives of notable men and women in comprehensive detail was sparked by the publication of Samuel Johnson's *An Account of the Life of Mr Richard Savage* in 1744. Today, look at any bestseller list and you'll find among it at least one book belonging to the genre.

Biography has even transcended the written form and found its way onto our screens with biopics, films which dramatize the true events of an individual's life, and biographical documentaries, such as Asif Kapadia's *Amy*, attracting an increasingly large following.

The biography is here to stay and in this chapter we will explore the reasons behind its success and longevity and develop a better understanding of why we should both read and write non-fiction of this variety.

What is a biography?

WHAT ARE THE CONVENTIONS OF A BIOGRAPHY?

- The Russian author Vladimir Nabokov called biographers 'psycho-plagiarists'

Put simply, a biography is a written account of someone's life. Although biographies usually take a narrative form, they are rooted in fact and based on actual real-life events, making them non-fiction texts.

A biography often proceeds chronologically through the stages of a person's life, frequently beginning at birth and, in many cases, ending with the death of the subject. In between, we become intimately acquainted with the details of the subject's life, both the mundane and the extraordinary, and emerge with an understanding of what makes this person significant. Biographies come in all sizes – they can range from full-length books that provide a comprehensive account of a person's life, to comparatively shorter biographical essays, which focus only on key experiences and events.

ACTIVITY: What are the conventions of a biography?

■ **ATL**

- Critical-thinking skills: Draw reasonable conclusions and generalizations

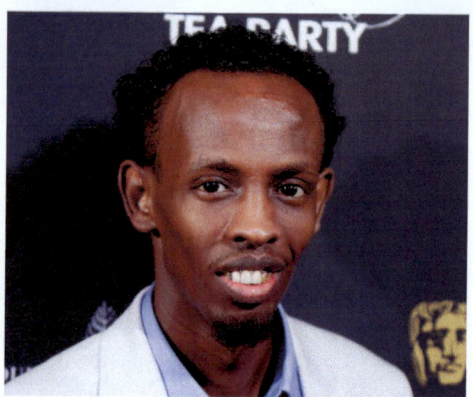

- *'I'm walking red carpets. Big celebrities recognize me. I never thought it would happen. It is just really unbelievable.'* Barkhad Abdi

BIOGRAPHY (www.biography.com) is a digital resource of over 7000 biographies about notable figures, past and present, from across the globe.

Read the biography of the actor Barkhad Abdi, opposite, taken from the website. Use the text to help you identify the conventions of biographical writing.

◆ **Assessment opportunities**

- In this activity you have practised skills that are assessed using Criterion A: Analysing.

Writers that track the life of a subject in narrative form are called biographers. The Russian author Vladimir Nabokov called biographers 'psycho-plagiarists' and according to Sigmund Freud, the founder of psychoanalysis, 'To be a biographer you must tie yourself up in lies, concealments, hypocrisies … ' What do you think Nabokov and Freud are suggesting about the nature of biographical writing? Is biographical writing truly a form of non-fiction? Or must we always add embellishments to cover up what we don't know, or perhaps what we do not wish to reveal, about our subject?

What information is being provided here? What does this add to the biography?

Why have these key events been included? What impact might they have on a reader?

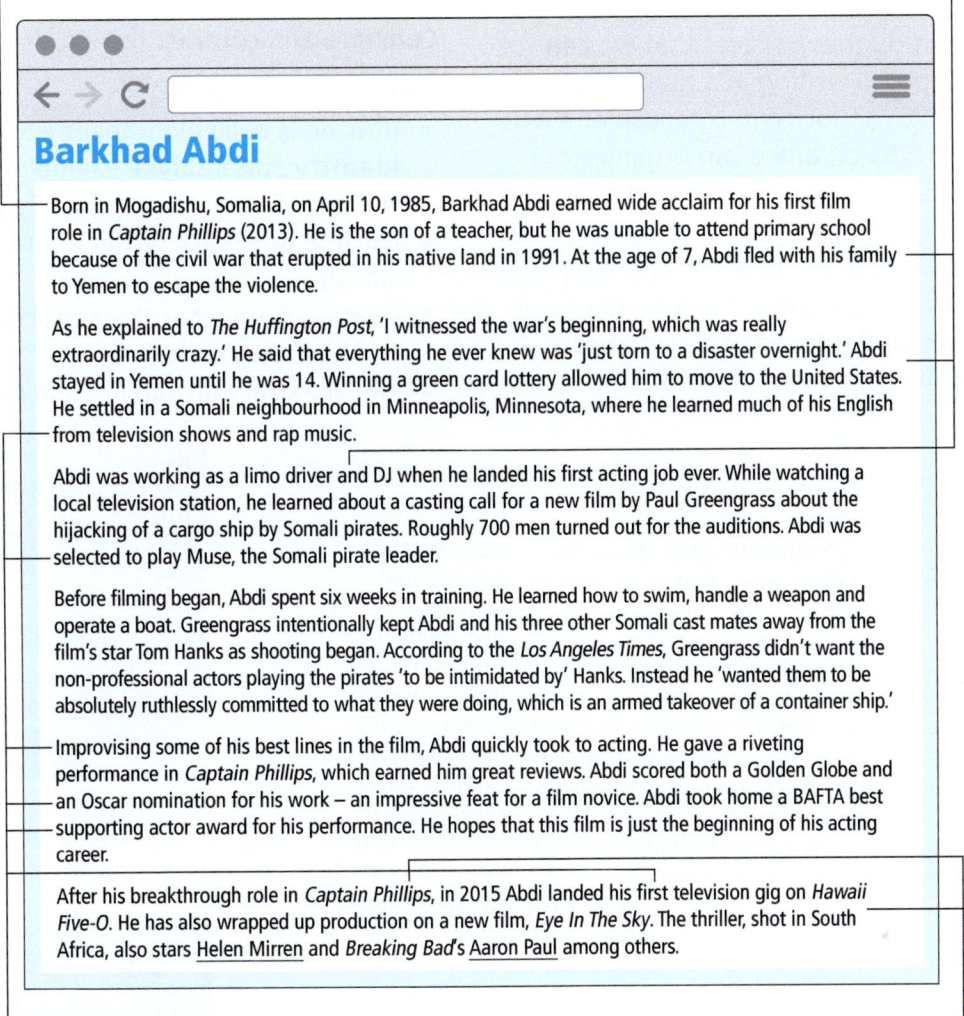

Barkhad Abdi

Born in Mogadishu, Somalia, on April 10, 1985, Barkhad Abdi earned wide acclaim for his first film role in *Captain Phillips* (2013). He is the son of a teacher, but he was unable to attend primary school because of the civil war that erupted in his native land in 1991. At the age of 7, Abdi fled with his family to Yemen to escape the violence.

As he explained to *The Huffington Post*, 'I witnessed the war's beginning, which was really extraordinarily crazy.' He said that everything he ever knew was 'just torn to a disaster overnight.' Abdi stayed in Yemen until he was 14. Winning a green card lottery allowed him to move to the United States. He settled in a Somali neighbourhood in Minneapolis, Minnesota, where he learned much of his English from television shows and rap music.

Abdi was working as a limo driver and DJ when he landed his first acting job ever. While watching a local television station, he learned about a casting call for a new film by Paul Greengrass about the hijacking of a cargo ship by Somali pirates. Roughly 700 men turned out for the auditions. Abdi was selected to play Muse, the Somali pirate leader.

Before filming began, Abdi spent six weeks in training. He learned how to swim, handle a weapon and operate a boat. Greengrass intentionally kept Abdi and his three other Somali cast mates away from the film's star Tom Hanks as shooting began. According to the *Los Angeles Times*, Greengrass didn't want the non-professional actors playing the pirates 'to be intimidated by' Hanks. Instead he 'wanted them to be absolutely ruthlessly committed to what they were doing, which is an armed takeover of a container ship.'

Improvising some of his best lines in the film, Abdi quickly took to acting. He gave a riveting performance in *Captain Phillips*, which earned him great reviews. Abdi scored both a Golden Globe and an Oscar nomination for his work – an impressive feat for a film novice. Abdi took home a BAFTA best supporting actor award for his performance. He hopes that this film is just the beginning of his acting career.

After his breakthrough role in *Captain Phillips*, in 2015 Abdi landed his first television gig on *Hawaii Five-O*. He has also wrapped up production on a new film, *Eye In The Sky*. The thriller, shot in South Africa, also stars Helen Mirren and *Breaking Bad*'s Aaron Paul among others.

Why does Abdi deserve a biography? What do we learn about his achievements?

How does the biography end? **Use** what you have learned so far in this chapter to **comment** on the structure of the biography.

Did you know …

… biographies don't always have to focus on the life of an individual? Over the years writers have produced biographies of collective groups of people, such as families, teams and bands; we can also find an abundance of biographies about places, movements and even ideas!

Do a quick search online to see if you can find examples of biographies which fall into these categories.

If you had to write a biography about an idea, what would you focus on? Discuss with a partner.

So now that we've got to grips with some of the conventions of biography writing, we can begin to think about how to get started.

ACTIVITY: Gripping your reader

ATL

- Communication skills: Read critically and for comprehension

Professor Kathryn Hughes believes that we can approach biographical writing in a number of different ways. We can focus on a particular event in the life of our subject, or we can organize our narratives around an object which might have been significant to the person we are writing about. We could take a 'life in parts' approach and only focus on a particular period in the life of our subject, for example the time they lived abroad. Some writers think that rather than looking at our subject in isolation, divorced from their social context, it is better to try and make sense of an individual's life by looking at them as part of a 'collective' and exploring their connections to others and their world around them.

Read the openings of the following biographies. **Compare and contrast** the extracts.

Consider the following:

- How does each biographer engage the audience? **Identify** and **analyse** examples of language or stylistic choices to help **justify** your opinion.
- **Outline** how each writer approaches their subject matter.
- **Comment** on what the extracts have in common and how they differ.
- Which extract do you like the most? Explain why.

> HAD Dr. Johnson written his own life, in conformity with the opinion which he has given, that every man's life may be best written by himself; had he employed in the preservation of his own history, that clearness of narration and elegance of language in which he has embalmed so many eminent persons, the world would probably have had the most perfect example of biography that was ever exhibited. But although he at different times, in a desultory manner, committed to writing many particulars of the progress of his mind and fortunes, he never had persevering diligence enough to form them into a regular composition. Of these memorials a few have been preserved; but the greater part was consigned by him to the flames, a few days before his death.
>
> *Life of Johnson*, James Boswell, 1791

■ Boswell's biography of Samuel Johnson is widely considered to be the first modern biography

> After the death of the great King, beautiful Versailles, fatal for France, lay empty seven years while fresh air blew through its golden rooms, blowing away the sorcery and bigotry which hung about the walls like a miasma, blowing away the old century and blowing in the new. Louis XIV died in 1715. He had outlived his son, his grandson and his eldest great-grandson, had reigned seventy-two years, too long for the good of his country. Even then he was so strong he could not die until half eaten away with gangrene, for which Dr. Fagon, killer of Princes, prescribed asses' milk. At last the Duc du Bouillon, wearing a black feather, went out on the balcony and announced to the waiting crowd, furious but not sad, 'Le Roi est mort'. He retired into the palace, put on a white feather, came back and announced 'Vive le Roi'.
>
> *Madame De Pompadour*, Nancy Mitford, 1954

■ Sometimes the life of the biographer is as interesting as the biographee! Nancy Mitford was already an established novelist before she began penning *Madame De Pompadour*. Mitford is best known for her semi-autobiographical post-war novels, *The Pursuit of Love* and *Love in a Cold Climate*.

On 25 February 1936, Jean Rhys boarded a French ship called the Cuba at Southampton Dock. The ship was bound for Dominica, her childhood home, which she had left twenty-nine years previously. Since then, she had lived in London, Paris and Vienna; she has married twice and given birth to two children (the first died in infancy, the second was living with her ex-husband). She had published a volume of short storied entitled *The Left Bank*, a translation of a French thriller, *Perversity*, and three novels, *Quartet*, *After Leaving Mr Mackenzie* and *Voyage in the Dark*. She had received critical acclaim, albeit somewhat guarded, and very little financial reward.

The Blue Hour: A life of Jean Rhys, Lilian Pizzichini, 2009

■ Jean Rhys is best known for her 1966 novel, *Wide Sargasso Sea*

I was never really wanted.

John Lennon was born with a gift for music and comedy that would carry him further from his roots than he ever dreamed possible. As a young man, he was lured away from the British Isles by the seemingly boundless glamour and opportunity to be found across the Atlantic. He achieved that rare feat for a British performer of taking American music to the Americans and playing it as convincingly as any home-grown practitioner, or even more so. For several years, his group toured the country, delighting audiences in city after city with their garish suits, funny hair and contagiously happy grins.

John Lennon: The Life, Phillip Norman, 2008

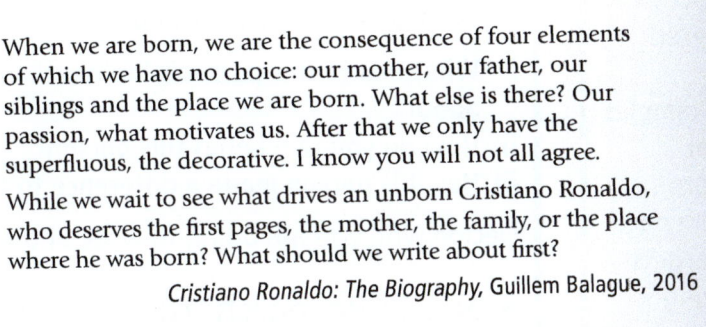

■ The Beatles singer and songwriter John Lennon was an icon to the young during the 1960s and 70s

When we are born, we are the consequence of four elements of which we have no choice: our mother, our father, our siblings and the place we are born. What else is there? Our passion, what motivates us. After that we only have the superfluous, the decorative. I know you will not all agree.

While we wait to see what drives an unborn Cristiano Ronaldo, who deserves the first pages, the mother, the family, or the place where he was born? What should we write about first?

Cristiano Ronaldo: The Biography, Guillem Balague, 2016

■ Cristiano Ronaldo. Footballers' lives are often a popular subject for biographies

◆ **Assessment opportunities**

◆ In this activity you have practised skills that are assessed using Criterion A: Analysing.

ACTIVITY: Asking the right questions

■ ATL

- Critical-thinking skills: Formulate factual, topical, conceptual and debatable questions
- Communication skills: Give and receive meaningful feedback
- Organization skills: Set goals that are challenging and realistic

Writing about a living subject means that there may be an opportunity to gather lots of great first-hand information. And what better way to do this than an interview?

1. **Create** a series of questions you could ask to acquire information about the life of your biographee. Think carefully about each one – good questions are the key to a good biography.
   You may want to learn about their childhood, family life, friendships and romantic relationships; it might be interesting to get their opinions on social issues and historical events that have taken place during their lifetime. What you really want is to understand what makes them tick, so get creative.
2. Join up with a partner and take turns to interview one another. Make sure you take detailed notes so you can use them later.
3. Now, use the information you have gathered about your partner to write the opening paragraph of a biography. Refer to the examples you have looked at already in this chapter.
4. Join with another pair, and this time share your paragraphs with the group. Evaluate each other's work and set yourselves some targets to help improve the quality of your writing.

◆ Assessment opportunities

- In this activity you have practised skills that are assessed using Criterion B: Organizing, Criterion C: Producing text and Criterion D: Using language.

ACTIVITY: Researching and writing a biographical essay – a guide

■ ATL

- Communication skills: Organize and depict information logically
- Information literacy skills: Access information to be informed and inform others; Evaluate and select information sources and digital tools based on their appropriateness to specific tasks
- Creative-thinking skills: Create original works and ideas

Follow the guidelines below to help you plan and write a biographical essay.

Stage 1: Plan!

On your own, create a mind map of famous people that you could use as subjects for your essay. These should be people you are fascinated by and want to learn more about. A biography is the best way to acquire new knowledge and become an expert in your field.

Evaluate your list, and narrow it down to just three candidates. Carry out a search on the internet to see how much information is available about the people you have selected. Ask yourself the following questions about each candidate to help you choose who to write about:

i   What makes this person's life worth writing about?
ii How do you feel about this person?
iii Has this person made a difference to the world?

Decide who you are going to write about.

Stage 2: Research, research, research!

This is quite possibly the most important stage of the process. You must ensure that as a biographer, you are honest, accurate and clear. A good knowledge of your subject will ensure that you meet these requirements.

In pairs, make a list of all the possible sources you can use to gather information from. Outline and evaluate the benefits and limitations of each of these sources and consider how you can overcome any obstacles.

You'll need at the very least to find out the basic facts about your subject, such as where and when they were born and where they lived during their lifetime.

Create a timeline to help you organize this information and where you can plot further details of key events and experiences.

Next, find out about the events which shaped your subject's life such as accomplishments, failures, obstacles and their contribution and legacy.

See if you can find primary as well as secondary sources; a biography can often benefit from the inclusion of quotations from the subject or their contemporaries.

Stage 3: Write!

Follow the tips below and aim to write 500–700 words. Make sure you organize your essay using paragraphs:

- **Introduction: Introduce your subject – who are you writing about and why should they be written about? Have an idea about what you want to focus on and make this clear at the start of your essay.**
- **Support your ideas with the information you have gathered as part of your research.**
- **Think about how you can use language and stylistic choices to engage your reader. You want to try and achieve an informative and lively tone.**
- **Give your essay a strong, cohesive conclusion. Relate it back to the points you made in your introduction.**
- **As you write, bear in mind the targets you set yourself on page 38.**

◆ Assessment opportunities

- ◆ In this activity you have practised skills that are assessed using Criterion B: Organizing, Criterion C: Producing text and Criterion D: Using language.

▼ Links to: Individuals and Societies/History

To some extent, biographers are required to take on the role of historians. Unearthing the story of someone's life takes a great deal of time, effort and extensive research. Historians, like biographers, rely on all sorts of resources when they are studying the past. These documents can be largely divided into two types of sources, primary and secondary.

Primary sources are documents or artefacts created during a particular period in history. Primary sources can include letters, diaries and photographs. They are important because they can reflect the individual perspective of a participant or observer at a certain point in time. Primary sources are valuable as they allow us to get really close to what might have happened in the past.

A **secondary source**, on the other hand, is a source of information that has been created by someone else who did not experience first-hand the events you are researching. Secondary sources can include books, newspapers, websites, and television or radio programmes.

Of course, we have to be careful when we use information of any kind – sometimes sources can provide us with a biased or one-sided viewpoint; they might not present information accurately; sometimes we need to ascertain whether the source is genuine or not before we can trust it.

When using or referring to information we haven't produced ourselves, it is essential that we acknowledge the sources appropriately by including footnotes or a bibliography (a list of texts that appears at the end of a book or essay).

Why should we read and write biographies?

WHAT CAN WE GAIN FROM READING BIOGRAPHIES?

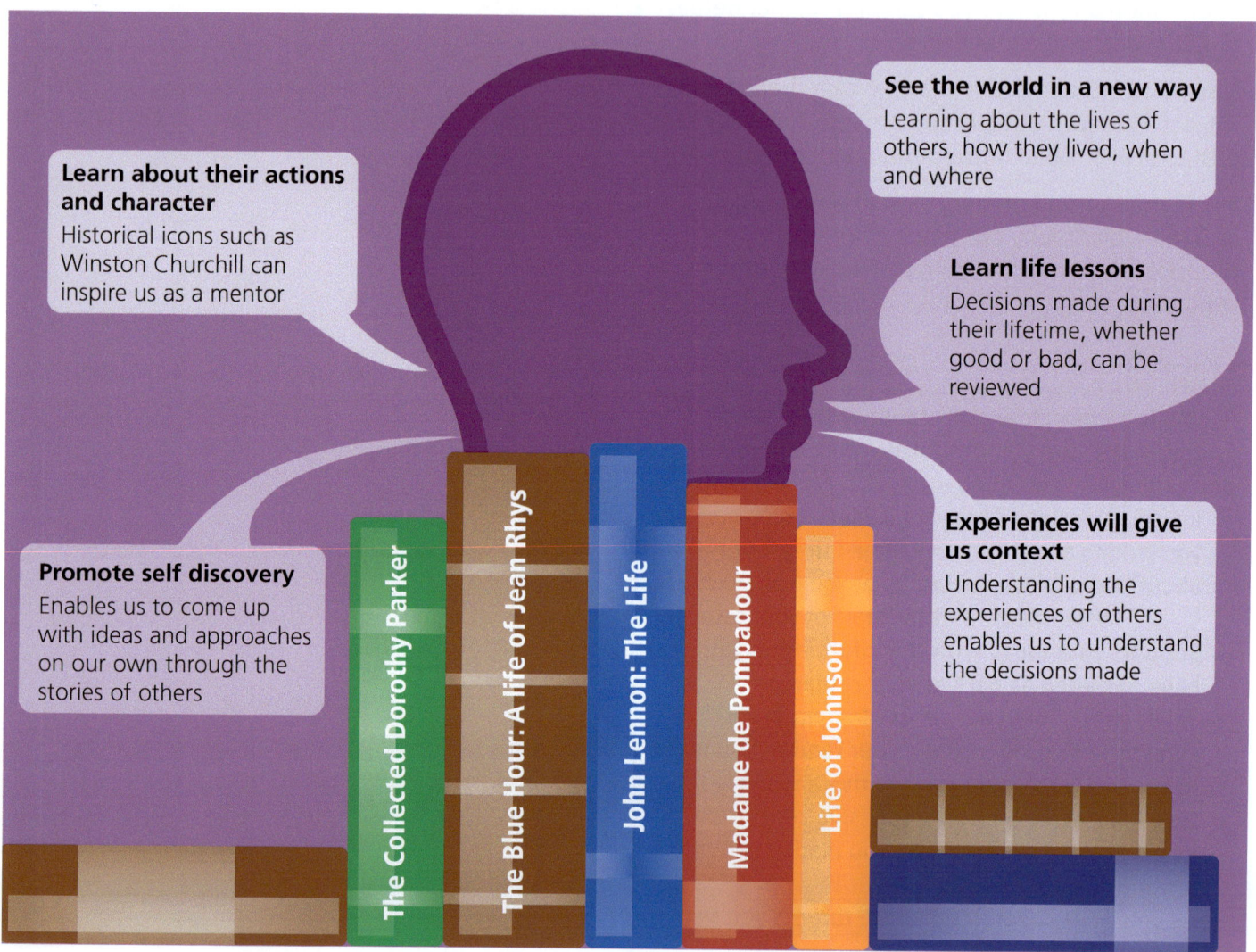

■ Biographies are much more than just 'a good read'! Here are just some of the reasons why we should read them.

Most people love a good story, and knowing that what we are reading is based on a real person's life experiences can make it all the more compelling. Sometimes life can be stranger than fiction and nowhere is this better captured than in the genre of biography. Perhaps this is why, since the eighteenth century, biographies have been consistently popular with the reading public.

But biographies are more than just a source of entertainment. Yes, they satisfy our natural, human, desire for gossip, but they also help us to understand ourselves and others better. Biographies teach us that human nature is complex and that in reality, people aren't as easily categorized as they can be in fiction. Real people are very rarely entirely good or entirely bad; we all have our virtues and we all have our flaws, and it can be reassuring when we recognize these aspects in our heroes in the pages of their biographies.

Not only do biographies provide us with an insight on human nature, but they can also be a source of inspiration, can help instil hope within us in times of adversity and give us a better understanding of the world of the past.

ACTIVITY: Biographers on biography

■ ATL

- Critical-thinking skills: Draw reasonable conclusions and generalizations

What inspires biographers to write? Let's find out from the experts themselves.

Antonia Fraser is an award-winning biographer who is best known for her books about Mary Queen of Scots and the six wives of Henry VIII.

Read the article over the page and complete the tasks which follow.

1 **Identify** what inspired Fraser to become a biographer.
2 What happened when she began to explore the topic introduced by Strachey independently? **Interpret** what she means by 'artistic truth'.
3 What was the initial impact of Strachey's work on Fraser?
4 **Summarize** what qualities Fraser believes a good biographer should possess.
5 According to Fraser, what mistakes are biographers prone to making?
6 What pleasures does she derive from writing biography?
7 In your opinion, what IB learner profile attributes do biographers need to possess?

◆ Assessment opportunities

- In this activity you have practised skills that are assessed using Criterion A: Analysing.

2 What makes a life worth writing about? 41

Step back in time

There's nothing like immersing yourself in a bygone era and bringing it to life, says historical biographer Antonia Fraser.

Gibbon was inspired to write *The Decline and Fall of the Roman Empire* sitting on the steps of the Capitol at Rome one evening, listening to the sound of monks chanting vespers. My own inspiration to become a historical biographer came in rather less elevated circumstances, as a teenager one rainy Oxford afternoon: I began to read Lytton Strachey's *Eminent Victorians*, and as a recent convert, was in particular fascinated by his essay on the worldly Cardinal Manning. This was going to be the life for me! Once back at school I plunged into further research in the convent library. A very different picture emerged. Gradually as I pursued the topic, I became aware of Strachey's daring sallies into 'artistic truth' (as opposed to historical truth). Nevertheless I never forgot my original sense of being transported into a world more vivid than my own.

An ability to convey this sensation is, I believe, at the heart of the matter. If you, the biographer, don't thrill to your subject, you can hardly in all fairness expect the reader to do so. In a sense (not of course the commercial sense) the choice of subject is irrelevant so long as it meets that requirement. You could say that I was extremely lucky to choose Mary Queen of Scots for my first foray since there proved to be a world-wide public for the troubles of the ill-fated Queen. But you could argue equally that I made my own luck, since I had always been obsessed by Mary's story from childhood. Nor was success fore-ordained. It was, after all, the leading publisher Mark Bonham-Carter of (then) Collins who said to me when I confessed my project, 'They say that all books on Mary Queen of Scots sell and no books on South America do', before adding with a laugh, 'Perhaps yours will be the exception.'

Nevertheless I did have luck. In the 60s, so-called narrative biography was said to be out of fashion. Mary Queen of Scots was an early beneficiary from the fact that the public continued to have an appetite for it, so long as the research was felt to be solid.

The actual research for a biography – now that's a whole other matter. The paramount need for it – historical truth not Stracheyesque truth must be established – means that biographers discover for themselves the reality of Dr Johnson's wise dictum about the greatest part of a writer's time being spent in reading in order to write: 'A man will turn over half a library to make a book.' And what about those fabled things boasted of on blurbs: hitherto unpublished documents? Obviously it is every researcher's dream to discover such papers, and their discovery once again may make a project commercial which would not otherwise be so.

There is also no excitement like that of viewing the piece of paper on which the subject actually wrote. The delicate white gloves now demanded by Conservation made it particularly exciting when I inspected the single surviving Wardrobe Book of Marie Antoinette in the Archives Nationales in Paris – to say nothing of the presence of armed gendarmes behind me, quite ready to defend this treasure of France to the death (mine).

At the same time I would issue a caveat about hitherto unpublished documents. HUDs are not in themselves more valuable than the printed sources – it's a historical coincidence that one set has become known early on, the other not. One needs to evaluate them even more closely. Here I speak from personal experience. A series of chances led me to discovering some hitherto unpublished letters of Oliver Cromwell just as I was finishing my manuscript. I blazoned my finds across the text: only to realise at the proof stage, that they might be unpublished but they were not very important in the grand scheme of things ... an expensive mistake.

Where the perils and pleasures of writing historical biography are concerned, there are two perils which seem to me to raise points of principle. The first is the peril of anachronistic judgements. For example, in the 16th century more or less everybody took astrology seriously and more or less everybody enjoyed a jolly afternoon out to see the bears baited. It's no good dismissing the former as meaningless and cringing from the latter as disgusting. In the same way, political correctness is dangerous. The importance of James I of England's allegedly homosexual tastes is their political consequences if any, not an opportunity for a 21st-century historian to display liberal values. (Let alone the reverse.)

I would further cite the peril of hindsight. We may know that Henry VIII will marry six times, but he didn't, and he would have been amazed if it had been predicted at the time of his first marriage to Catherine of Aragon.

And the pleasures? Manifold! Principal among them however is the opportunity to lead a life less ordinary. As a biographer, I can rule over kingdoms, lead the cavalry into battle, patronise the great artists of the past and all without leaving my chair.

ACTIVITY: 'They say'

■ **ATL**

- Communication skills: Make inferences and draw conclusions; Read critically and for comprehension

Read the extract taken from James West Davidson's biography of journalist and activist Ida B. Wells (opposite), and complete the tasks. For each task, **use** evidence from the text to **justify** your response.

1 **Identify** key facts the writer includes about Ida B. Wells.
2 What opinions does the writer hold about his subject?
3 **Evaluate** how successfully the writer weaves historical context into his biography.
4 **Summarize** what you learn about the world in which Ida B. Wells lived.
5 Explain how this information influences your feelings towards Ida B. Wells.
6 How important do you think it is to consider the subject's world when writing their biography? Explain why.

◆ Assessment opportunities

- In this activity you have practised skills that are assessed using Criterion A: Analysing.

Fact or opinion

Biographers frequently mix fact and opinion in their work, so as readers, it is important for us to be able to distinguish between the two.

A **fact** is something that is known and has been proven to be true. Facts can be verified and backed up by evidence. For example: *Henry VIII married six times*.

An **opinion** is a view or judgment about something, which can't really be checked. For example: *Henry was the most handsome king in Europe in his day*.

Compare and contrast the two statements and identify the differences between the two. What do you notice about the language used to express the opinion?

For more on **fact and opinion**, visit:

https://bbc.in/3pe5qll

In 1881, Miss Ida B. Wells belonged to none of these professions. She was a teacher and proud of it, even if the work could be frustrating. Her pupils addressed her as Miss Wells, as did her male and female colleagues. That was a badge of freedom, after all. For two hundred years, whites had called adult slaves by their first names, as if they were still children, or bestowed patronizing names like Cuffee and Cicero. Like other middle-class folk, if Wells went visiting and no-one was home, she left a calling card, with her name engraved as she preferred it: Miss Ida B. Wells.

Moving to Memphis, Ida obtained a job at a school in Woodstock, a town a dozen miles north of the city. Every week she got to classes by riding the Chesapeake, Ohio and Southwestern Railroad. The C&O schedules were regular enough. But it was hard to anticipate from week to week the reception she might receive on board the train.

A lot depended on which car she rode. Trains usually pulled two. The one directly behind the engine was the smoking car, also known as second class, where conditions were far from ideal. Tobacco fumes filled the air and those riders who chewed instead of smoked habitually ignored the spittoons and showered the floor with tobacco juice. Nor was smoke the only pollutant. Because the car sat directly behind the locomotive, engine ash and soot were much more likely to drift in the doors. In winter, heat was provided by a wood stove whose legs were screwed down and sides braced against the wall, to keep hot coals from jostling onto the floor. In summer, a difficult choice had to be made: whether to shut the windows and suffocate or open them and be showered by cinders.

Since the smoker held the cheapest seats, the people using them were often a rougher crowd. Tobacco was the least of the vices to be endured, for men bought along pints of whiskey and amply indulged their thirsts. Swearing and arguing were common. 'The cars were jammed, all the way over here, with the dirtiest, nastiest set I ever rode with,' complained one traveler. Immigrant families with baggage also crowded in, travelling on discounted rates.

First-class accommodations could be had in what was known as the ladies' car. Men were sometimes permitted if they maintained a proper decorum and did not smoke, though often they were also escorting a woman. Most of these cars boasted a water cooler, carpets on the floor, and upholstered seating. The surroundings were desirable enough that one male passenger, travelling alone, sued the railroad after being refused a seat in first class. The foul air in the smoker was likely to make him ill, he insisted.

For Ida the choice was clear: buy first class tickets. But whether she could use them was a question that had increasingly become complicated in the early 1880s. Leaving her lodgings at Aunt Fannie's she could catch a streetcar to the railroad depot, sitting side by side with whites without arousing any remark or protest. Streetcars were integrated in major Southern cities beginning after the war.

So far in this chapter we have explored the conventions of biographical writing and considered some of the reasons why people write and, indeed read, texts of this genre. We have also developed an understanding of the importance of good research and have had a go at planning and writing our own biographical essays.

What makes a life worth writing about?

Every life has a story, but what makes that story worth transcribing? Should only the lives of the famous be documented? Do readers today care only for tales of success? Or is it only those whose lives are fraught with difficulties that deserve to be immortalized in writing? And what about the lives of ordinary people? Do their stories matter? Why should we read them?

In his award-winning book *Stuart: A Life Backwards*, Alexander Masters not only breaks the rules that most biographers follow by subverting time and telling Stuart's story 'backwards', beginning with his death and ending with his early life, he takes for his subject an ordinary man. By narrating the details of Stuart's troubled life, Masters forces us to confront issues such as homelessness, substance abuse and crime, and restores dignity to a man who throughout his life had been perceived by society as more a problem rather than a person.

Masters proves to us that it is not just the lives of those in the public eye that are interesting enough to fill the pages of a biography; ordinary lives can be extraordinary in their own way too!

ACTIVITY: Whose lives do we want to read about?

■ ATL

- Collaboration skills: Negotiate effectively; Listen actively to other perspectives and ideas
- Critical-thinking skills: Consider ideas from multiple perspectives

Visit your local bookstore or browse the internet for a list of biographies. In groups, look at the list of careers in the table opposite.

Copy the table and in the last column note down approximately how many biographies about people in each career category you came across in your initial search. Carry out another search and see if you can fill in any gaps.

Discuss which of the careers are valued most by our society. How does society show their appreciation for these professionals? How are they rewarded; how are they celebrated?

Rank the careers in order of how much they are valued. For example, place the most valued at number 1, and the least at 20. You must come to an agreement about this rank order as a group, so make sure you can justify your reasons to one another.

Do the same for the next column, but this time evaluate the contribution you think professionals from each field make to society.

Did you know …

… an obituary is a notice of a person's death published in a newspaper? An obituary consists of a brief biography of the deceased. The word 'obituary' comes from the Latin *obit,* meaning death, and has been used to refer to published death notices since the eighteenth century.

To see some examples you can visit the links below:

www.nytimes.com/section/obituaries

www.theguardian.com/tone/obituaries

■ An obituary typically includes a brief biography of the deceased person

Career/Profession	Value	Contribution	Biographies (Number? Titles?)
Footballer			
Nurse			
Pop-star			
Politician			
Teacher			
Fire officer			
Writer			
Actor			
Doctor			
Model			
Police officer			
Royal			
Scientist			
Refuse collector			
Social media influencer			
Banker			
Judge			
Entrepreneur			
Activist			
Television presenter			

Once you have completed the table as a group, take some time to reflect on what you have learned during this activity.

What have you discovered about who biographers frequently make the subjects of their writing? What is your opinion about this?

♦ **Assessment opportunities**

♦ In this activity you have practised skills that are assessed using Criterion B: Organizing.

2 What makes a life worth writing about?

Can a writer or artist's biography give us a better understanding of their work?

When you pick up a book you'll often find that it contains a brief author biography outlining the writer's achievements or giving a brief summary of their life. But how important is it for us to know about a writer's life for us to enjoy their work? Does knowing about their experiences or their relationships with others enhance our understanding and appreciation of the themes they tackle in their writing? The same could be said for artists of any kind.

In some cases, the biography of the writer or artist is so inextricably linked to their work that it is impossible to avoid making connections as a reader. Take Jean Rhys for instance; once a reader is acquainted with the facts of her life, it is difficult to read her novels and short stories without interpreting her female protagonists as literary incarnations of herself.

In the 1940s, some literary critics suggested that we focus on the close reading of a text rather than on the author's life or intentions and this idea prevailed for some time. What do you think? Should writing be separated from the writer? Discuss in pairs.

Register and formality

When we talk about '**register**', we are referring to how we change the way we speak or write to suit our purpose or the context we are in.

This includes the degree of formality and the choice of lexis (vocabulary) used.

Language linked to a particular topic or subject is called the **semantic field**. For example, words such as black, blue, pink, turquoise and gold all make up the semantic field of colour.

We can consider register on a sliding scale:

from an informal, casual register → to a highly formal & sophisticated register

An informal text may...

- Contain high frequency, **monosyllabic lexis** – these are shorter words, usually made up of a single **syllable**, which appear frequently in a single text. For example, *the*, *it*, *you*.
- Consist of **simple and compound sentences**.
- Contain **colloquial language**.

A formal text may ...

- Contain low frequency, **polysyllabic lexis** – these are longer words made up of two or more syllables, which appear less frequently in a text: For example, *patriotic*, *parsimonious*, *elegant*.
- Include **jargon** – these are topic-specific words which may only be understood by subject specialists. For example, *beneficiary*, *arbitration*, *indemnity* or *ancillary relief* are examples of legal jargon which a non-specialist may find inaccessible.

ACTIVITY: Author biography

ATL

- Communication skills: Read critically and for comprehension
- Critical-thinking skills: Draw reasonable conclusions and generalizations

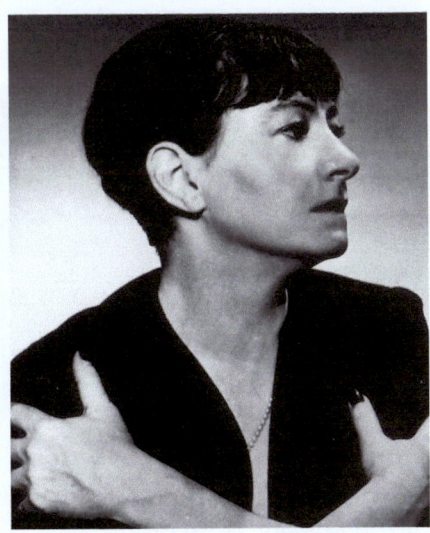

■ Dorothy Parker was known for her scathing wit

Look at the example below of an author biography taken from *The Collected Dorothy Parker*.

Read it and complete the following tasks:

1 How would you describe the register of this text? Use evidence from the text to **justify** your answer.
2 Can you **identify** any semantic field/s in the text? How might this be related to the context and purpose of the text?
3 **Identify** examples of polysyllabic lexis. How many of these words can you define? Use the context of the sentence the words appear in to try and guess the definition. Check your answers using an online dictionary.

◆ Assessment opportunities

- ◆ In this activity you have practised skills that are assessed using Criterion A: Analysing and Criterion B: Organizing.

Dorothy Parker was born in West End, New Jersey, in 1893 and grew up in New York, attending a Catholic convent school and Miss Dana's School in Morristown, New Jersey. In 1916 she sold some of her poetry to the editor of *Vogue*, and was subsequently given an editorial position on the magazine, writing captions for fashion photographs and drawings. She then became drama critic of *Vanity Fair* and the central figure of the celebrated Algonquin Hotel Round Table.

Famous for her spoken wit, she showed the same trenchant commentary in her book reviews for the *New Yorker* and *Esquire* and in her poems and sketches. Her collections of poems included *Not So Deep as a Well* and *Enough Rope*, which became a bestseller; and her collections of stories included *Here Lies*. She also collaborated with Elmer Rice on a play, *Close Harmony*, and with Arnaud d'Usseau on the play *The Ladies of the Corridor*. She herself had two Broadway plays written about her and was portrayed as a character in a third. Her cynicism and the concentration of her judgments were famous, and she has been closely associated with modern urbane humour.

Her first husband was Edwin Pond Parker II, and although they were divorced some years later, she continued to use his name, which she much preferred to her own of Rothschild. Her second husband was an actor-writer, Alan Campbell. They went to Hollywood as a writing team and went through a tempestuous marriage until his death in 1963, when Dorothy Parker returned to New York. She died in 1967.

EXTENSION

Do you want to develop your vocabulary? Wish you knew more polysyllabic words? The Merriam Webster online dictionary is a great place to start.

Visit the link and try the quiz. www.merriam-webster.com/word-games/vocabulary-quiz.

As part of the game, you must match a specified word to a **synonym**. Once you have completed the quiz, review your answers and use the dictionary function to look up the definition of the words you didn't know.

Write down your new words in a notebook, with definitions and an example sentence for each to help you remember how to use the words in context.

Set yourself a target to use some of your new words in conversation throughout the day.

ACTIVITY: Does art imitate life?

ATL

- Communication skills: Read critically and for comprehension
- Information literacy skills: Access information to be informed and inform others
- Critical-thinking skills: Evaluate evidence or argument

Look at the texts on pages 51 and 52.

To begin, read the texts without finding out any information about the writers. Note down your initial impressions of the texts and discuss them with a partner.

Now, **use** the internet to carry out some research about the writers and complete the following tasks:

1 Find connections between what is depicted and the biographies of the writers.
2 Does knowing more about the writer's life enhance your enjoyment of each text? Does this in any way deepen your intellectual grasp of the texts? Discuss in pairs.
3 In your opinion, should we make connections between the biography of the writer and the texts they produce? Discuss with a partner.

◆ Assessment opportunities

- ◆ In this activity you have practised skills that are assessed using Criterion A: Analysing.

After breakfast, Adèle and I withdrew to the library, which room, it appears, Mr. Rochester had directed should be used as the schoolroom. Most of the books were locked up behind glass doors; but there was one bookcase left open containing everything that could be needed in the way of elementary works, and several volumes of light literature, poetry, biography, travels, a few romances, &c. I suppose he had considered that these were all the governess would require for her private perusal; and, indeed, they contented me amply for the present; compared with the scanty pickings I had now and then been able to glean at Lowood, they seemed to offer an abundant harvest of entertainment and information. In this room, too, there was a cabinet piano, quite new and of superior tone; also an easel for painting and a pair of globes.

I found my pupil sufficiently docile, though disinclined to apply: she had not been used to regular occupation of any kind. I felt it would be injudicious to confine her too much at first; so, when I had talked to her a great deal, and got her to learn a little, and when the morning had advanced to noon, I allowed her to return to her nurse. I then proposed to occupy myself till dinner-time in drawing some little sketches for her use.

Jane Eyre, Charlotte Brontë, 1847

I, Too

I, too, sing America.

I am the darker brother.
They send me to eat in the kitchen
When company comes,
But I laugh,
And eat well,
And grow strong.

Tomorrow,
I'll be at the table
When company comes.
Nobody'll dare
Say to me,
'Eat in the kitchen,'
Then.

Besides,
They'll see how beautiful I am
And be ashamed—

I, too, am America.

I, Too, Langston Hughes, 1926

> ! **Take action: Opportunity to apply learning through action …**
>
> ! **Celebrate the lives of inspiring historical figures at your school:** On a weekly basis, celebrate the life of a person selected by a class in your school. You could get together and write a brief biography of their life and display it around your school.
>
> ! **Explore biographies online:** You can find thousands of biographies on this website. Read a biography or watch a video. Go on, have a browse: www.biography.com
>
> ! **Write the biography of an ordinary person:** Acknowledge someone's achievements by putting them in a biography! You could write the story of a friend, a parent, one or both of your grandparents, a neighbour or someone who has made a contribution to your local community. Biographies take a lot of research though, so start by interviewing your chosen person – you might want to record it using a Dictaphone or on your phone (ask their permission first!) so you don't miss any of the crucial details. Then get writing!
>
> ! **Live a life worth writing about:** Take Pessl's advice and *'always live your life with your biography in mind.'* Be inspired by the stories of others and live your life in the way that you want to!

Mother blows her nose in a daintily embroidered cambric handkerchief and taking the doctor's hand, presses it to her eyes. Father sniffs and clears his throat.

'What about her schooling?' he asks, masking his emotion. I can't tell if he is inordinately pleased by the condition of my leg – or inordinately disappointed.

'She's doing fine without school, isn't she?' says the doctor. 'Don't pressure her … her nerves could be affected. She doesn't need to become a professor.' He turns to me. 'Do you want to become a professor?'

I shake my head in a firm negative. 'She'll marry – have children – lead a carefree, happy life. No need to strain her with studies and exams,' he advises, thereby sealing my fate.

Mother's mouth is again working – her eyes again brimming. And driven by unfathomable demons, again her guilt surfaces. 'I don't know where I went wrong,' she says. 'It's my fault … I neglected her – left her to the care of ayahs. None of the other children who went to the same park contracted polio.'

'It's no one's fault really,' says Colonel Bharucha, reassuring her as usual. 'Lenny is weak. Some child with only the symptoms of a severe cold could have passed the virus.' And then he roars a shocking postscript: 'If anyone's to blame, blame the British! There was no polio in India till they brought it here!'

Cracking India, Bapsi Sidhwa, 1988

A SUMMATIVE PROBLEM TO TRY

Use this problem to apply and extend your learning in this chapter. This task is designed so that you can evaluate your learning using the Language and Literature criteria.

Task: *Alfred Hitchcock: A Brief Life*

Read the extract over the page from Peter Ackroyd's biography of the prolific director Alfred Hitchcock and complete the task.

Present your answers in full sentences and ensure that you use evidence from the text to support your ideas.

You have 60 minutes to complete this task.

1 **Identify** elements typical of biography writing that Ackroyd uses in the extract.
2 What details does the writer include to add authenticity to his writing? **Comment** on the effect of this.
3 How would you describe the register of this text? **Justify** your response using evidence from the text.
4 How does Ackroyd use language and stylistic choices to engage readers?
5 **Write two PEA paragraphs** about how Ackroyd builds up a picture of Alfred Hitchcock through focusing on his work.

■ Ivor Novello as the eponymous lodger of Hitchcock's adaptation of Marie Belloc Lowndes' novel

■ Sir Alfred Hitchcock, 'the Master of Suspense'; a life worth writing about

2 What makes a life worth writing about?

In February 1926 Gainsborough Pictures announced that the star of *The Lodger* was to be Ivor Novello, a matinee idol whose previous career both as a composer of musical comedies and romantic lead of silent films did not necessarily prepare him for the role of a suspected killer of women. By the end of the story, of course, he would have to be vindicated, but Hitchcock was good at compromise.

In March he began what he called variously 'the first real Hitchcock film' or 'my first picture,' with its combination of Victorian melodrama and expressionistic techniques. He and his cameraman were at one in preferring shafts of light and intense shadows, sudden close-ups and vertiginous staircases. The story was a simple one: at the time of a series of killings, a mysterious stranger arrives at the Bunting household in search of lodgings. The camera roams through the Bunting house as if it were intent upon laying a ghost, but the atmosphere of suspense and suspicion has already been very carefully established. The film opens with the face of a screaming woman, a device Hitchcock would use again as an emblem of female hysteria and sexuality, and then the night sky of London is punctured by a neon sign announcing 'To-Night Golden Curls.'

Enter Novello from the London fog like a wraith; the gas lamps of the house flicker and dim as he crosses the threshold into the Bunting world of cosy domesticity. The lower part of his face is covered. The eyes do all the work. To today's audiences it might look like overacting, but at the time it was simply intensity. He is led up to his rooms on the second floor, and at once the staircase becomes one of the themes of *The Lodger*; it might be seen as an image of spiritual mystery, mounting ever higher, but it also prompts the fear of falling. In one of the most technically expert scenes, lasting no more than ten seconds, Hitchcock turns a ceiling into glass so that the Buntings can actually see the pacing footsteps of their lodger; this effect would have come as a shock to contemporary audiences. At the end of the film the lodger, known as 'The Avenger,' is pursued by a ferocious London mob and is suspended by handcuffs from a set of railings. Hitchcock always liked handcuffs.

The filming took six weeks, but Hitchcock sensed trouble even before the first screening. There were still whispers of resentment against him at Gainsborough Pictures, orchestrated in part by Graham Cutts who could not forgive his erstwhile assistant's rise in the company. Cutts had as an ally the chairman of the distribution company attached to Gainsborough, C. M. Woolf. Both men believed that Hitchcock's experimental techniques would alienate an English audience. 'I don't know what he's shooting,' Cutts told someone at the studio. 'I can't make head or tail of it.' He prophesied disaster.

Neither Hitchcock nor Alma [his wife] attended the formal screening in front of Woolf and others. Instead they trudged the stones of London together for an hour and a half. Both of them were praying, since Alma had just been on a Catholic induction course in preparation for her marriage. They were eventually greeted, on their return, to devastating news. *The Lodger* was declared to be a fiasco, too 'arty' and too 'highbrow.' It would have to be shelved. Hitchcock's career looked as if it might be over just after it had begun.

Reflection

In this chapter we have we developed an understanding of the conventions of the **genre** of biographical writing. Through reading biographies we have learned about how writers use language and stylistic choices to **communicate** and preserve individual histories. In addition, through carrying out research for our own biographies, we have gained a better understanding of the social and historical **contexts** that may have influenced the lives of the people we are writing about. Most importantly, we have seen how biographies have the power to inspire and how they can help shape our **identities and relationships**.

Use this table to reflect on your own learning in this chapter.						
Questions we asked	Answers we found	Any further questions now?				
Factual: What is a biography? What is a biopic?						
Conceptual: Why should we read biographies?						
Debatable: What makes a life worth writing about? Can a writer or artist's biography give us a better understanding of their work?						
Approaches to learning you used in this chapter:	Description – what new skills did you learn?	How well did you master the skills?				
		Novice	Learner	Practitioner	Expert	
Thinking skills						
Communication skills						
Research skills						
Collaboration skills						
Organization skills						
Learner profile attribute(s)	Reflect on the importance of inquiry for our learning in this chapter.					
Inquirer						

Connections | **Theme; Character** | **Identities and Relationships**

3 Why do we need to belong?

Filmmakers use the medium of film to make **connections** with their audiences and to explore **themes** that shed light on how our **relationships** with others can help shape our individual **identities**.

CONSIDER AND ANSWER THESE QUESTIONS:

Factual: What is whānau? What is foster care?

Conceptual: How can film help us to understand other cultures? How can films be used to critique social injustice? Why should we express our feelings? Why do we need to belong? What can we gain from our relationships with others? How can we cope with loss?

Debatable: How can we tackle social inequality? Does the media glamourize gang culture?

Now **share and compare** your thoughts and ideas with your partner, or with the whole class.

IN THIS CHAPTER, WE WILL ...

- **Find out** about the culture and history of New Zealand.
- **Explore** how film can be used to highlight issues of importance.
- **Take action** to raise awareness about the social issues addressed in *Hunt for the Wilderpeople*.

■ **These Approaches to Learning (ATL) skills will be useful …**

- Communication skills
- Collaboration skills
- Thinking skills
- Research skills
- Critical-thinking skills
- Affective skills
- Organization skills

● **We will reflect on this learner profile attribute …**

- Caring – We show empathy, compassion and respect.

◆ **Assessment opportunities in this chapter:**

- Criterion A: Analysing
- Criterion B: Organizing
- Criterion C: Producing text
- Criterion D: Using language

ACTIVITY: Discussion

In this chapter you will be exploring a visual text, a film, which has been adapted from a novel. To begin, in a group, discuss the following questions:

1 Have you seen any film adaptations of books that you have read?
2 How faithful to the original text were these films? Did you like or dislike them?
3 What challenges do you think filmmakers face when adapting books for the screen?
4 What elements should a book have that would make it ideal for film adaptation?
5 Should we appreciate the films as creative works in their own right, or must we consider them in relation to the book?
6 If you could make a film of any book of your choice, what would you choose and why?

KEY WORDS

Māori   neologism
indigenous   flora
foster care   fauna
bereavement

How can film help us to understand other cultures?

WHAT IS THE PURPOSE OF FILM?

Ever since the advent of the first motion picture cameras in the late-nineteenth century, film has had an enthralling power over audiences across the globe. Films are much more than just a source of entertainment; they can be used to transmit powerful messages, to move, to inspire, and perhaps most importantly, to teach.

Films, like books, can transport readers into worlds they have never encountered, or in some cases, never even imagined. Films provide audiences with an all-encompassing sensory experience – they engage not just our sense of sight, but also our sense of sound, dimension, and now with the recent development of 4-D cinema, even our sense of touch. Cinema is not just immersive, but for some it is a more accessible way of exploring issues often tackled in literature.

Through character and setting we can experience empathy for others and begin to understand the customs, traditions and values of people from other places and other communities. Watching films also allows us to explore what it is that connects us, whilst simultaneously celebrating our cultural differences.

In this chapter, through a study of Taika Waititi's film *Hunt for the Wilderpeople*, we will explore how films can help us to develop a better understanding of other cultures, and how they can be used to raise awareness of important social issues.

ACTIVITY: Book to film

■ ATL

- Communication skills: Make inferences and draw conclusions

Visit the link and listen carefully to the review on the 'Book to Film' podcast from ABC Australia. Complete the tasks.

http://mpegmedia.abc.net.au/rn/podcast/2016/06/bay_20160604_1446.mp3

1 **Identify** the differences between the film and the book. What has the director changed? What has he retained?
2 **Infer** why the director might have made these changes.
3 What does the term 'Pākehā' mean?
4 What do you learn about the point of view the story is told from in the book?

■ *Hunt for the Wilderpeople* is director Taika Waititi's adaptation of Barry Crump's 1988 novel, *Wild Pork and Watercress*.

5 **Summarize** what you learn about the author of the novel, Barry Crump.
6 What do you learn about the animals used in the film? **Interpret** what this reveals about New Zealanders' attitudes to their environment.
7 Where is the film set? What do you learn about the setting?
8 How does the filmmaker appeal to both local and global audiences?
9 Based on what you've heard, what themes do you think are explored in this film?

◆ Assessment opportunities

- In this activity you have practised skills that are assessed using Criterion A: Analysing.

EXTENSION
Author and director biographies

Use the internet to find out more about the life of **author Barry Crump** and **director Taika Waititi**.

Think back to some of the ideas you explored in Chapter 2. Does knowing more about the writer of the novel and the director of the film enhance your appreciation of *Hunt for the Wilderpeople*? **Discuss** in pairs.

■ Barry Crump

■ Taika Waititi

Writing reviews

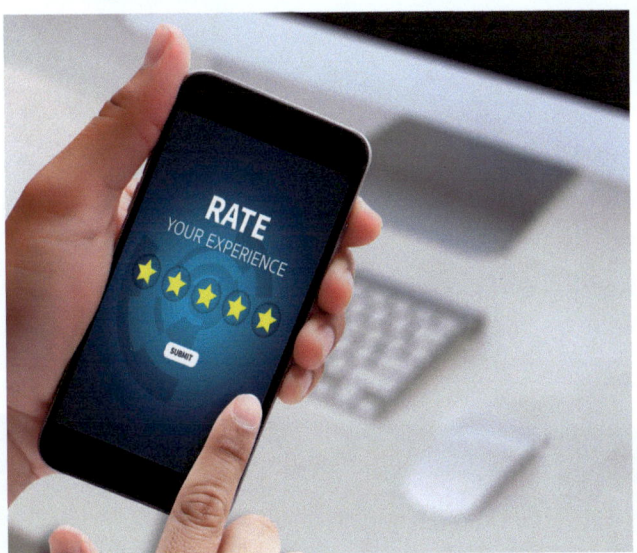

A review is critical article, report or podcast, evaluating a book, play, concert, film or work of art. A review can also be about a restaurant, an attraction or experience.

Reviews are often organized chronologically and the conventions can differ depending on the subject of the piece. The **tone** of a review is often lively and conversational and the first paragraph can sometimes be used to introduce a certain 'angle' the writer is taking, for example the background of the director or the media's treatment of an artist.

Listen again to the review and see if you can identify any of the following conventions:
- Evaluative adjectives.
- Opinion disguised as fact.
- Facts and background information (reviews are often well researched).
- Direct quotations – what do you think these add to a review?
- Narrative voice – reviews can be written in first or third person narrative voice.
- Informal or colloquial vocabulary (written reviews often contain elements of spoken language).
- A variety of sentence lengths and types.
- Topic-specific vocabulary.
- Descriptive language.

Explore further by using the internet to find some written reviews.

3 Why do we need to belong?

■ 'We got to shoot in some places that no one else has ever filmed in before. I think it's probably the most fun I've had on a shoot, just in terms of being outside in quite extreme conditions. But it was also really rewarding, in the sense that I didn't spend a lot of time – definitely not in the last decade – appreciating our country.' Taika Waititi

ACTIVITY: Setting – New Zealand

ATL

- Communication skills: Read critically and for comprehension
- Information literacy skills: Access information to be informed and inform others

Task 1

In pairs, create a mind map about all that you know about New Zealand. What do you associate with the place? Can you find it on the world map?

Use the internet to find out more about New Zealand and create a country profile. You may want to find out about the following:
- **Key information: capital city; population.**
- The country's history – you may want to present this as a timeline.
- The landscape and environment (New Zealand is home to lots of unique flora and fauna).
- The languages spoken.
- Culture – customs and traditions; major festivals.
- Notable people – activists, writers, artists.

Task 2

In *Hunt for the Wilderpeople*, the majority of the action takes place out in the New Zealand bush, or 'te ngahere' as the Māori call it. This is an area of outstanding natural beauty, but, as Ricky very quickly realises, a difficult terrain to navigate. Early on in the film, Ricky incorrectly refers to the bush as the 'jungle', but in the 1840s the word 'bush' was used as a synonym for 'jungle' by Europeans who found the bush hard to travel through.

The compiler of this Guide has journeyed through our marvellous Maoriland from the far North even to its farthest South. He has seen and felt some of the might the majesty of loveliness of our glorious lakes girt about with bush-clad hills, of snow-capped mountains frowning through the clouds, of our sublimely noble fjords, in all their solitary grandeur. The beauty born of murmuring sound has oftimes charmed his ear, and his soul has not been wholly insensible to those awe-inspiring evidences of volcanic power, our geysers, fumaroles, and boiling springs.

Yet when he would fain write of these myriad prodigies of 'our Good Mother Nature,' when he would clothe the 'thoughts that breathe' in the 'words that burn,' he is painfully conscious of the truth of Byron's lines from *The Bride of Abydos*:

> Who hath not proved how feebly words essay
>
> To fix one spark of beauty's heavenly ray?

Fully recognising the impotence of mere words to convey any idea of the splendid magnificence of this wondrous country, the writer has caused the letterpress to be copiously interspersed with illustrations, which will speak much more eloquently to the reader.

The day will come to many who see this guide in Europe, Great Britain, America, or Australia, when they will say:

> 'Tomorrow to fresh woods and pastures new'

When this time arrives, those who let the 'fresh woods and pastures new' be those of New Zealand, will assuredly say if they follow the course laid down in this book, 'The half was never told.'

In conclusion, the advice which the compiler of this admittedly faulty and imperfect work would give to his readers, is that which the Delphic Oracle gave to Polycrates, as the best means of finding a treasure buried by Xerxes' general, Mardonius, on the field of Plataea, 'turn every stone'.

Historically, the bush has also been associated with rebellion. The bush was seen as the preserve of Māori guerrilla fighters during the New Zealand wars, who fought to oppose its destruction and subsequent conversion to farmland. You can find out more about this later. The bush therefore, is an appropriate setting for Ricky to act out his defiance of the system that seeks to separate him from his new home.

Read C. N. Baeyertz's introduction above to his 1902 tourist guide to New Zealand and complete the following tasks:

1 Use an online dictionary to find out the definition of any words you don't understand.
2 How would you describe the writer's attitude to New Zealand? **Identify** the words in the text which best convey this attitude.
3 **Identify** an example of the each of the following in the text:
   a personification
   b hyperbole
   c onomatopoeia
   d adverb
   e alliteration
   f abstract noun
   g adjective
4 **Analyse** the lines from Lord Byron that the writer quotes. Explain why Baeyertz has chosen this quotation and what message he is trying to convey.
5 **Interpret** what he means by the advice he leaves the reader at the end of the extract.

3 Why do we need to belong?

■ The exquisitely beautiful landscapes of New Zealand have attracted tourists since the nineteenth century

ⓘ Did you know …

… that New Zealand was the first self-governing country in the world where women won the right to vote?

Thanks to efforts by suffrage campaigners like Kate Sheppard, the Governor, Lord Glasgow, signed a new Electoral Act on the 19th September 1893. Women in other parts of the world, including Britain and America, were not granted this right until after the First World War.

■ In the early 1890s, Kate Sheppard and her peers compiled a series of massive petitions calling on Parliament to grant the vote to women.

Writing chapters

A chapter is a main division of a book that typically has a number and/or a title. The latter often relates to the main topic that might be addressed in that particular portion of the book. In non-fiction texts this makes the content easier for the reader to navigate. The word 'chapter' is also used to describe a certain phase or period in a person's life.

Although many modern books are no longer organized in chapters, you'll find that most writers still choose to write with them. Why? Let's find out!

1. **Pacing and dramatic impact:** Chapters can be used to control the pace at which your narrative progresses and can be used to keep your readers on edge. Ending a chapter with a cliffhanger can be a great way of creating suspense.

2. **Point of view:** Chapters can allow a writer to shift from one character's point of view to another. In Part 3 of his bestselling novel *A Thousand Splendid Suns*, Khaled Hosseini uses alternating chapters to convey the perspectives of his two female protagonists, who find themselves sharing a house and a husband.

3. **Time:** Chapters also allow you to play with time; a writer can switch from past to present or just skip periods of time in which nothing significant occurs.

4. **Tradition:** In the nineteenth century, novels were published in serialized form in magazines over a longer period of time. When these serials or episodes were eventually bound together in book form, these divisions naturally became chapters.

Although *Hunt for the Wilderpeople* is not a book, it *is* structured using chapters. Why do you think the director has adopted this structure? What impact might it have on the audience?

Did you know …

… the term 'cliffhanger' is thought to have come from Thomas Hardy's 1873 novel *A Pair Of Blue Eyes*? In one serialized edition, Hardy left one of his protagonists, Henry Knight, literally hanging off a cliff!

ACTIVITY: The film

ATL

- Media literacy skills: Demonstrate an awareness of media interpretation of events and ideas
- Communication skills: Make effective summary notes for studying

Copy the table below, and as you watch the film note down the titles of each of the ten chapters. Pause at the beginning of each chapter to briefly summarize key events which have taken place in the previous chapter. You can use the final column in the table to note down anything else you find of interest (quotations; observations about characters; setting).

Chapter title	Chapter summary	Other
1.		
2.		
3.		
4.		
5.		
6.		
7.		
8.		
9.		
10.		

3 Why do we need to belong?

Why do we need to belong?

WHAT CAN WE GAIN FROM OUR RELATIONSHIPS WITH OTHERS?

■ The secret to our longevity as a species may well be down to our social instincts

SELF-ACTUALISATION
morality, creativity, spontaneity, acceptance, experience, purpose, meaning and inner potential

SELF-ESTEEM
confidence, achievement, respect of others, the need to be a unique individual

LOVE AND BELONGING
friendship, family, intimacy, sense of connection

SAFETY AND SECURITY
health, employment, property, family and social ability

PHYSIOLOGICAL NEEDS
breathing, food, water, shelter, clothing, sleep

■ Maslow's hierarchy of needs

In 1943, the psychologist Abraham Maslow came up with the theory that in order to fulfil our potential as individuals, we must achieve certain needs. He suggested that some needs take precedence over others and created a five-stage model, a 'hierarchy of needs', to illustrate this. According to Maslow, once the needs of the first stage (our basic human need for food, shelter, sleep) are met, then only can we develop new needs, and so on until we achieve self-actualisation, or put simply, the fulfilment of our individual talents. For Maslow, the human need to belong is essential to our personal development, and he ranks it third in the hierarchy.

Humans are social creatures and it seems that we thrive on interacting with others; this is why we like spending time with people around us, whether that be friends, family or members of our local community. But is this an inherent part of human nature or something we have developed over time?

For our ancestors, 'sticking together' and belonging was tantamount to survival. Whether it was because it meant safety in numbers, or because working together to hunt, gather and grow food was a more efficient way of living, the secret to our longevity as a species may well be down to our social instincts.

But belonging, and feeling as though we are a part of something greater, is more than just a means of survival. Feeling as though we belong gives our lives meaning and can play a crucial role in shaping our identity. Through our relationships with others we can learn to make sense of the world around us and develop empathy for others; if we can learn to love others and be loved in turn, then we can learn to value ourselves more as individuals.

By far the greatest benefit of belonging is having an external support network; an individual or perhaps a group of people that we can turn to in times of difficulty.

> Next morning we drove for several hours to Barry's place in Opotiki. It wasn't legal or ethical, but the nine-year-old drove while Barry sat in the passenger seat, telling the rest of us that it was more nerve-wracking for him than it was for his young driver, Coonch. There was one brief stop, just before we reached Barry's, when Coonch ordered the dog up a bank next to the road. A minute or two later, very pleased with himself, the dog emerged with a possum clenched in his jaws: dinner was sorted. Coonch casually drove on down a bank, over a river and onto Barry's property, where we stayed for several days.
>
> When Barry started talking – that voice like gravel – we all listened intently as we knew we were in the presence of one of the great storytellers. Coonch was no different from the rest of us – he was mesmerised. But if Barry ever motioned there was something needing attention outside or an adventure around the corner, his sidekick and now best mate was instantly right there by his side.

ACTIVITY: Ricky Baker

■ ATL

- Communication skills: Make inferences and draw conclusions; Read critically and for comprehension

Ricky Baker is the protagonist of the story. In Crump's novel, the story is told from Ricky's point of view through the use of a first person narrative.

According to Martin Crump, the novelist's son, Ricky is based on a real person, Coonch, a nine-year-old Māori boy, who he describes as his father's 'sidekick'. In a preface for his father's book, Martin recounts a story from his childhood.

1. What similarities can you **identify** between Coonch and the character of Ricky Baker?
2. What did Martin Crump realize when they sat listening to Barry's stories?
3. In the film, what challenges does Ricky face when he tries to settle into Bella and Hec's household?
4. In the film, how does the director create sympathy for Ricky? Support your ideas with evidence from the film.
5. **Outline** the impact Bella has on Ricky.
6. What IB learner profile characteristics does Ricky possess and develop over the course of the film? **Discuss** first in pairs and then **create** a learner profile for Ricky. **Use** quotations from the film as examples to support each point.

◆ Assessment opportunities

- In this activity you have practised skills that are assessed using Criterion A: Analysing, Criterion B: Organizing and Criterion D: Using language.

ACTIVITY: The biography of Ricky Baker

■ ATL

- Creative-thinking skills: Create new works and ideas

Cast your mind back to what you learned about biographical writing in the previous chapter. In pairs, remind yourself about what makes a good biography.

Write a 500-word biography about Ricky Baker's life and experiences. Use quotations and details from the film to enrich your writing.

◆ Assessment opportunities

- In this activity you have practised skills that are assessed using Criterion B: Organizing, Criterion C: Producing text and Criterion D: Using language.

ACTIVITY: What is foster care?

■ ATL

- Critical-thinking skills: Draw reasonable conclusions and generalizations
- Collaboration skills: Practise empathy

Paula Hall is undoubtedly presented as the villain in Waititi's film. When we first encounter her, she describes Ricky as 'a real bad egg' while he is within earshot.

- What impact might this have on a child?
- **Interpret** what the director is suggesting about the way in which Paula, and indeed Child Services, the institution she represents, perceive children like Ricky.
- During her television interview, **identify** the metaphor Paula uses to describe Ricky. **Comment** on how it contradicts her 'no child left behind' motto.
- Re-watch the scenes which feature Paula. Which IB learner profile characteristics does she lack?

Abandonment is one of the themes the film explores. This, along with abuse and neglect, is one of the issues which can lead to children being placed in care. Ricky Baker represents just one of thousands of children in foster care around the world.

In the UK alone, nearly 64 000 children live with almost 55 000 foster families. Use the internet to find out **how many children live in foster care in New Zealand** and **in your home country**.

Foster care is a way of providing a family life for children who cannot live with their own parents. The experiences of foster children vary considerably – some children have incredibly positive experiences, while others, like Ricky before he is placed with Bella, aren't so lucky and find themselves moved from place to place, leaving them feeling unsettled and unwanted.

Visit the link to read about the experiences of people who have grown up in foster care:

www.theguardian.com/commentisfree/2016/feb/12/our-lives-in-foster-care-what-it-feels-like-to-be-given-a-new-family

ACTIVITY: Whānau

■ **ATL**

- Communication skills: Make inferences and draw conclusions

The Māori word 'whānau' is often translated as 'family', but it extends beyond this; social unity and a sense of community is an important part of the Māori culture so the word is often used to refer to friends or members of the wider community.

In pairs discuss the following questions:

1 How is the concept of whānau explored in the film?
2 Which characters don't seem to 'belong', particularly early on in the film?
3 What message does the director want to convey about the notion of belonging? How is this message reinforced by the ending? Where does Ricky find acceptance in the end? What connects him to the people he finds a home with?
4 Collate a list of quotations from the film about the theme of family and keep it safe. You will need to refer to it later.
5 What does Ricky gain from his relationship with Hec?

◆ **Assessment opportunities**

♦ In this activity you have practised skills that are assessed using Criterion A: Analysing.

ACTIVITY: *The Canary*

■ **ATL**

- Collaboration skills: Practise empathy
- Communication skills: Read critically and for comprehension

Katherine Mansfield is one of New Zealand's most celebrated writers. She is best known for her short stories.

Read her story on the next page and complete the tasks that follow.

1 **Identify** the narrative voice the story is told in.
2 How old do you think the narrator is? Support your answer with evidence from the text.
3 What is the significance of the canary and its song to the narrator?
4 What themes are addressed in the story?
5 How does Mansfield create sympathy for the narrator? **Identify** and **analyse** language and stylistic choices used by the writer.
6 Can you make any connections between Mansfield's protagonist and any of the characters from *Hunt for the Wilderpeople*?
7 A recent survey revealed that almost three-quarters of older people in the UK are lonely. How does this make you feel? Visit the link to find out more and see how you can help:

https://www.campaigntoendloneliness.org/facts-and-statistics/

◆ **Assessment opportunities**

In this activity you have practised skills that are assessed using Criterion A: Analysing.

! Take action

! In pairs, discuss how your school could engage elderly people in your local community to help them overcome feelings of loneliness and to give them a sense of belonging.

3 Why do we need to belong?

The Canary

YOU see that big nail to the right of the front door? I can scarcely look at it even now and yet I could not bear to take it out. I should like to think it was there always even after my time. I sometimes hear the next people saying, 'There must have been a cage hanging from there.' And it comforts me; I feel he is not quite forgotten.

You cannot imagine how wonderfully he sang. It was not like the singing of other canaries. And that isn't just my fancy. Often, from the window, I used to see people stop at the gate to listen, or they would lean over the fence by the mock-orange for quite a long time—carried away. I suppose it sounds absurd to you—it wouldn't if you had heard him—but it really seemed to me that he sang whole songs with a beginning and an end to them.

For instance, when I'd finished the house in the afternoon, and changed my blouse and brought my sewing on to the veranda here, he used to hop, hop, hop from one perch to another, tap against the bars as if to attract my attention, sip a little water just as a professional singer might, and then break into a song so exquisite that I had to put my needle down to listen to him. I can't describe it; I wish I could. But it was always the same, every afternoon, and I felt that I understood every note of it.

I loved him. How I loved him! Perhaps it does not matter so very much what it is one loves in this world. But love something one must. Of course there was always my little house and the garden, but for some reason they were never enough. Flowers respond wonderfully, but they don't sympathise. Then I loved the evening star. Does that sound foolish? I used to go into the backyard, after sunset, and wait for it until it shone above the dark gum tree. I used to whisper 'There you are, my darling.' And just in that first moment it seemed to be shining for me alone. It seemed to understand this something which is like longing, and yet it is not longing. Or regret — it is more like regret. And yet regret for what? I have much to be thankful for.

But after he came into my life I forgot the evening star; I did not need it any more. But it was strange. When the Chinaman who came to the door with birds to sell held him up in his tiny cage, and instead of fluttering, fluttering, like the poor little goldfinches, gave a faint, small chirp, I found myself saying, just as I had said to the star over the gum tree, 'There you are, my darling.' From that moment he was mine.

It surprises me even now to remember how he and I shared each other's lives. The moment I came down in the morning and took the cloth off his cage he greeted me with a drowsy little note. I knew it meant 'Missus! Missus!' Then I hung him on the nail outside while I got my three young men their breakfasts, and I never brought him in until we had the house to ourselves again. Then, when the washing-up was done, it was quite a little entertainment. I spread a newspaper over a corner of the table and when I put the cage on it he used to beat with his wings despairingly, as if he didn't know what was coming. 'You're a regular little actor,' I used to scold him. I scraped the tray, dusted it with fresh sand, filled his seed and water tins, tucked a piece of chickweed and half a chilli between the bars. And I am perfectly certain he understood and appreciated every item of this little performance. You see by nature he was exquisitely neat. There was never a speck on his perch. And you'd only to see him enjoy his bath to realise he had a real small passion for cleanliness. His bath was put in last. And the moment it was in he positively leapt into it. First he fluttered one wing, then the other, then he ducked his head and dabbled his breast feathers. Drops of water were scattered all over the kitchen, but still he would not get out. I used to say to him, 'Now that's quite enough. You're only showing off.' And at last out he hopped and, standing on one leg, he began to peck himself dry. Finally he gave a shake, a flick, a twitter and he lifted his throat— Oh, I can hardly bear to recall it. I was always cleaning the knives at the time. And it almost seemed to me the knives sang too, as I rubbed them bright on the board.

Company, you see—that was what he was. Perfect company. If you have lived alone you will realise how precious that is. Of course there were my three young men who came in to supper every evening, and sometimes they stayed in the dining-room afterwards reading the paper. But I could not expect them to be interested in the little things that made my day. Why should they be? I was nothing to them. In fact, I overheard them one evening talking about me on the stairs as 'the Scarecrow.' No matter. It doesn't matter. Not in the least. I quite understand. They are young. Why should I mind? But I remember feeling so especially thankful that I was not quite alone that evening. I told him, after they had gone out. I said 'Do you know what they call Missus?' And he put his head on one side and looked at me with his little bright eye until I could not help laughing. It seemed to amuse him.

Have you kept birds? If you haven't all this must sound, perhaps, exaggerated. People have the idea that birds are heartless, cold little creatures, not like dogs or cats. My washerwoman used to say on Mondays when she wondered why I didn't keep 'a nice fox terrier,' 'There's no comfort, Miss, in a canary.' Untrue. Dreadfully untrue. I remember one night. I had had a very awful dream—dreams can be dreadfully cruel—even after I had woken up I could not get over it. So I put on my dressing-gown and went down to the kitchen for a glass of water. It was a winter night and raining hard. I suppose I was still half asleep, but through the kitchen window, that hadn't a blind, it seemed to me the dark was staring in, spying. And suddenly I felt it was unbearable that I had no one to whom I could say 'I've had such a dreadful dream,' or—or 'Hide me from the dark.' I even covered my face for a minute. And then there came a little 'Sweet! Sweet!' His cage was on the table, and the cloth had slipped so that a chink of light shone through. 'Sweet! Sweet!' said the darling little fellow again, softly, as much as to say, 'I'm here, Missus! I'm here!' That was so beautifully comforting that I nearly cried.

And now he's gone. I shall never have another bird, another pet of any kind. How could I? When I found him, lying on his back, with his eye dim and his claws wrung, when I realised that never again should I hear my darling sing, something seemed to die in me. My heart felt hollow, as if it was his cage. I shall get over it. Of course. I must. One can get over anything in time. And people always say I have a cheerful disposition. They are quite right. I thank my God I have. All the same, without being morbid, and giving way to—to memories and so on, I must confess that there does seem to me something sad in life. It is hard to say what it is. I don't mean the sorrow that we all know, like illness and poverty and death. No, it is something different. It is there, deep down, deep down, part of one, like one's breathing. However hard I work and tire myself I have only to stop to know it is there, waiting. I often wonder if everybody feels the same. One can never know. But isn't it extraordinary that under his sweet, joyful little singing it was just this—sadness?—Ah, what is it?—that I heard.

The Canary, Katherine Mansfield, 1922

How can films be used to critique social injustice?

So far in this chapter we have learned about some aspects of New Zealand's history, geography and culture and have developed an understanding of the conventions of review writing. Also, on viewing *Hunt for the Wilderpeople*, we have explored the themes of family, belonging and abandonment and considered ways in which we can engage isolated members of our local communities.

CAN FILMS CHANGE THE WAY WE SEE THE WORLD?

'Storytelling through film can be a powerful tool to engage audiences,' says Sheila Leddy, Executive Director at The Fledgling Fund, a foundation dedicated to bringing pressing social issues to light through cinema. And there's no denying it; film has the power to 'inform, inspire, and hopefully ignite social change.' You can find out more about the The Fledgling Fund by visiting the link and watching the video.
www.thefledglingfund.org

The far-reaching impact of film can give a voice to the voiceless, humanize those who have been marginalized, stereotyped, vilified, or simply misunderstood, and force us as viewers to confront the problems which plague our global community today. Throughout *Hunt for the Wilderpeople*, Waititi uses a mixture of comedy and drama to explore social issues and to critique the injustices which exist in New Zealand today.

Amongst the issues the film tackles are bereavement, social inequality, adult illiteracy and attitudes towards children in care. In this section we will take a closer look at some of these issues and consider how we can play a role in helping to tackling them.

ACTIVITY: Trouble in paradise – social inequality and race relations

■ ATL

- Critical-thinking skills: Evaluate evidence or argument; Gather and organize relevant information to formulate an argument
- Communication skills: Make inferences and draw conclusions; Write for different purposes
- Collaboration skills: Listen actively to other perspectives and ideas

Some critics suggest that *Hunt for the Wilderpeople* can be used to examine the complicated racial politics of New Zealand.

Māori, the ethnic group Ricky belongs to, are the indigenous people of New Zealand. The word 'indigenous' describes people or things which are native to a place. In the film, Ricky imagines himself to be a Māori freedom fighter, Te Kooti, defending the land against British soldiers. You can find out more about New Zealand's colonial past in the *Links to …* section opposite.

Although modern New Zealand society is progressive and inclusive, Waititi uses his film to show us that the ideas about certain groups of people, in this case young Māori men, still prevail. Just think back to the way Paula speaks about Ricky.

Ricky tells Hec that 'there's no more homes – only juvy.' 'Juvy' (juvenile detention) is part of the judicial system. The prison system in New Zealand today is part of the country's colonial legacy – historically, Māori who resisted British occupation were incarcerated by those in power. In New Zealand, Māori now make up a higher proportion of all new prisoners than at any time in recorded history.

In pairs discuss the following questions:

1. How far do you agree with critics that the film could be a critique of racial inequality in New Zealand?
2. How is Ricky dehumanized or vilified by others in the film? Find evidence to support your answer.
3. How do the authorities respond to Ricky running away? Is their reaction appropriate or disproportionate? Why do you think Waititi has chosen to present it in this way?
4. Is racism still a problem today? What is done to tackle racial inequality in your country? Does your country have a colonial past? Does this past have an impact on people's lives today? You might need to use the internet to find out more.
5. What do you think are the causes of racism? What are the consequences? Create a poster persuading people to put an end to racism. You can find a quick refresher on persuasive writing on this page.

◆ Assessment opportunities

- In this activity you have practised skills that are assessed using Criterion A: Analysing, Criterion B: Organizing, Criterion C: Producing text and Criterion D: Using language.

Persuasive writing: A refresher

The **purpose** of **persuasion** is to get someone to change their viewpoint about a certain issue or to get someone to act in a way in which you want them to.

So how can we be persuasive when we write? Here are some ideas:

- Address your audience by using **personal pronouns** – **I, you, we, us, our**. This engages your audience directly and can make them feel included and sometimes responsible. For example: *We all need to take part in the fight against climate change.*
- **Flatter** your audience and make them feel important. For example: *A successful company like yours understands the needs of their customers.*
- Make deals by using **conditional sentences**; this will make your audience feel that they have something to gain. For example: *If we use the bins provided, we will have a cleaner and more pleasant school environment.*
- Use **rhetorical questions** – questions which do not require an answer but are designed to make your audience or reader think. For example: *Can you imagine a world without war?*
- Make sure you provide justification and detailed support for your ideas. Sometimes **facts** and **statistics** can help show your reader that you know what you are talking about.
- **Repetition** of certain words and phrases can be very effective as it makes your **message** more memorable. For example: in Martin Luther King's famous speech, he repeats the phrase **'I have a dream'** eight times.

▼ Links to: Individuals and Societies/History

Visit the link provided here to access Te Ara: The Encyclopedia of New Zealand; this is a wonderful online resource that you can use to find out about the country's history.

https://teara.govt.nz/en/history

You can also learn more about New Zealand's efforts to eliminate racism here: https://teara.govt.nz/en/anti-racism-and-treaty-of-waitangi-activism

3 Why do we need to belong?

Does the media glamourize gang culture?

ACTIVITY: The 'skux' life

ATL

- Critical-thinking skills: Draw reasonable conclusions and generalizations
- Communication skills: Take effective notes in class
- Media literacy skills: Demonstrate an awareness of media interpretation of events and ideas

'I didn't choose the skux life, the skux life chose me,' declares Ricky Baker before driving a pickup truck into a corrugated iron fence.

Visit the link and listen to Julian Dennison, who plays Ricky in the film, explaining some New Zealand slang.

https://bit.ly/3c1W6DD

Hunt for the Wilderpeople is permeated with references to rap music and gang culture. Ricky names his pet dog after his favourite rapper and 'best friend', Tupac Shakur; he is fascinated by guns and is impressed by Hec's criminal past.

In the film, this creates humour and the treatment of the subject is playful. However, the reality of gang culture is rather more sinister. Gang-related violence devastates lives and wreaks havoc on communities. Often it is the young and vulnerable who fall victim to crimes perpetrated by gang members.

Listen to the podcast from Precious Lives, a series about young people and gun crime. The project is dedicated to raising awareness about the problem that afflicts so many communities in the US. As you listen, take notes on what you learn about the impact of gang culture.

- **Does what you have learned help you understand why being a 'gangster' might appeal to someone like Ricky?**
- **Do the media, film and music industries glamourize gang culture? In groups, carry out some research. Use the information you gather to debate the issue as a class.**

◆ Assessment opportunities

◆ In this activity you have practised skills that are assessed using Criterion A: Analysing.

Motifs

A **motif** is a recurring element in a literary text or film. A motif can be a symbol, a stylistic choice, an image, object, word, or spoken phrase within a film that points to a theme.

- Are there any particular words or phrases which are repeated in the film? Who uses them? What is their significance?
- Books and hot water bottles frequently appear throughout the film. Which themes can you relate these objects to? What do they symbolize? Are they associated with any characters in particular? Discuss with a partner.

ACTIVITY: Adult illiteracy

ATL

- Communication skills: Make inferences and draw conclusions
- Collaboration skills: Practise empathy

1. In 'Chapter Three, Goodbye Ricky Baker', what does Ricky learn about Hector? Comment on Ricky's reaction to this news. Is it appropriate?
2. How does Hec feel about his shortcomings?
3. What do you know about adult illiteracy? Discuss what you know with a partner and consider what factors might lead to adult illiteracy. What barriers are created by not being able to read? Use the link to find out more: www.fondationalphabetisation.org/en/causes-of-illiteracy/
4. What percentage of adults can't read in your home country? Use the internet to find out.
5. Has Hec's inability to read had a great impact on his life and relationships? What skills does Hector have that make up for this shortcoming?
6. What changes for Hector by the end of the film? What do you think inspires him to overcome the obstacle of reading? Organize your response in a paragraph and use evidence from the film to support your answer.

Why should we express our feelings?

HOW CAN WE COPE WITH LOSS?

When Ricky tells Hec that 'it's healthy to get these feelings out', he's on to something big! Although it can be daunting sometimes to talk about how we feel – whether we're sad, upset or angry – it's better to open up and share rather than battle with things on our own. Laying bare our souls can make us feel exposed and vulnerable, but the benefits most definitely outweigh the negatives.

Bottling up our emotions can make us behave differently and we can become withdrawn, disengaged and even resentful. Burying our anger or sadness can make us feel more alone, and unable to overcome the obstacles we're facing. Sharing the burden can be the first step towards resolving an issue and can make us feel better, even if what we are sharing can seem ugly.

Dealing with the loss of a loved one can feel like the hardest thing in the world sometimes. Around the world, people have different ways of dealing with bereavement and the grief that comes with it. In times like these, we should turn to family and friends to help us; knowing that there's someone out there simply to listen can help us to cope better.

But it's not just negative emotions we should be discussing; sharing positive thoughts and feelings can strengthen your relationships with others. If someone has made a difference to your life or helped you in some way, don't be afraid to tell them how grateful you are. Ultimately, speaking openly about how you feel will make you a better person and will give you the satisfaction of being open, honest and authentic.

ACTIVITY: What happens if we bury our feelings?

■ ATL

- Communication skills: Read critically and for comprehension

We have already encountered the work of William Blake in this book – you can refresh your memory by flicking back to page 14 in Chapter 1.

Read the poem below and complete the tasks.

1. **Define** wrath.
2. **Interpret** the message Blake is trying to convey.
3. **Identify** and **analyse** the stylistic choices Blake uses to convey this message.
4. **Explain** how the poem makes you feel.
5. Which character in *Hunt for the Wilderpeople* could benefit most from Blake's message? **Justify** your answer by making reference to the film.

◆ Assessment opportunities

- In this activity you have practised skills that are assessed using Criterion A: Analysing.

A Poison Tree

I was angry with my friend;
I told my wrath, my wrath did end.
I was angry with my foe:
I told it not, my wrath did grow.

And I waterd it in fears,
Night & morning with my tears:
And I sunned it with smiles,
And with soft deceitful wiles.

And it grew both day and night.
Till it bore an apple bright.
And my foe beheld it shine,
And he knew that it was mine.

And into my garden stole,
When the night had veild the pole;
In the morning glad I see;
My foe outstretched beneath the tree.

ACTIVITY: Haiku

ATL

- Communication skills: Read critically and for comprehension

In the film, Ricky uses haikus to express his thoughts and feelings – a technique he has picked up from a counsellor.

A **haiku** is a Japanese poem which consists of three lines and seventeen **syllables**. Traditionally, nature or the seasons are the subjects explored in poems of this type.

Here is one of Ricky's earlier haikus:

In a haiku, each line has a set number of syllables. There should be five syllables in the first line.

The second line of a haiku should always have seven syllables.

> **Maggots**
> There's heaps of maggots –
> Maggots wriggling in that sheep
> Like moving rice. Yuck.

The third and final line of a haiku repeats the syllable pattern of the first line and should contain five syllables.

What feelings is Ricky using his haiku to express? What inspires this haiku during his discussion with Bella?

Let's look at one of Ricky's later haikus. Read it in pairs and complete the following tasks:

> *Trees, birds, rivers, sky*
> *Running with my uncle Hec.*
> *Living forever.*

1 **Compare and contrast** the two haikus and **analyse** what they reveal about how Ricky has changed and developed over the course of the film.
2 Consider the language and **imagery** used in the second poem. Explain how this fits in with the conventions of traditional haikus.
3 **Interpret** the message of Ricky's haiku.

♦ Assessment opportunities

♦ In this activity you have practised skills that are assessed using Criterion A: Analysing.

■ Blake's poem warns about the consequences of not expressing our feelings

EXTENSION
Senryu

Senryu is an informal style of haiku, sometimes known has 'human haiku' which follows the same structure of the traditional poem, but doesn't limit the poet to writing about nature or the seasons; instead, it can be used to express emotion or to comment on human nature.

In pairs, evaluate whether Ricky's poems are more 'senryu' than 'haiku' in content.

Visit the link below to find out about the trend for senryu that swept Japan in the mid-1990s.

http://articles.latimes.com/1996-10-13/news/mn-53502_1_modern-japan

Have a go a writing your own haiku or senryu.

ACTIVITY: 'Walking, walking, trying to get somewhere'

■ **ATL**

- Affective skills: Managing state of mind (emotional management)
- Communication skills: Make inferences and draw conclusions

What inspires Ricky to call himself and Hec 'wilderpeople'? Wilderpeople is a neologism, a newly coined word or expression.

Hec and Ricky are a pair of misfit explorers out in the bush, who don't seem to have a destination in mind; they are just 'trying to get somewhere'. What they don't realize is that they're not just on a physical journey, but also a metaphorical one.

In pairs, answer the following questions:

1 Why doesn't Hec express his feelings openly? What is the source of his sadness and anger?
2 What do we learn about Māori death rituals? What does Bella tell Ricky about the lake that 'wets the cloak of the sky'? Identify the literary device she uses.
3 What do we learn about Ricky's experience of loss? How does this help him empathize with Hec?
4 What experiences give Hec closure following Bella's death?
5 Discuss what you know about death and mourning rituals in your country or culture. Why do we have such customs?

◆ **Assessment opportunities**

◆ In this activity you have practised skills that are assessed using Criterion A: Analysing.

! **Take action: Opportunity to apply learning through action ...**

! **Raise awareness about some of the issues we've explored in this chapter:** Shocked by the statistics about adult illiteracy? Saddened by the number of elderly people who experience loneliness? Enraged by the number of deaths caused by gang-related crime? Frustrated about the problems caused by racism in your community? Take action! Raise awareness by making posters, organizing charity events and inviting in external speakers. Ask a teacher to help you.

! **Express yourself through writing:** Feeling angry, sad or maybe even ecstatic? Write it out! Get yourself diary where you can write down your thoughts and feelings. Or take a page out of Ricky's book and write a haiku. Poetry can be a great outlet for emotion. And if you're really feeling down, remember: you don't have to deal with things alone. Speak to someone. Find out if your school offers a counselling service.

! **Watch more films!:** Set up a film club at your school. You could arrange lunchtime screenings or get people to watch the same film at home and then get everyone to record or write their own reviews.

SOME SUMMATIVE PROBLEMS TO TRY

Use these problems to apply and extend your learning in this chapter. These tasks are designed so that you can evaluate your learning using the Language and Literature criteria.

Task 1: Dear Diary

Write a diary entry or monologue from the perspective of Hec from *Hunt for the Wilderpeople*.

You should aim to write 500–700 words.

You have 60 minutes to complete this task.

Task 2: Essay

Write an essay-style response to the following question:

Explore the way in which the director presents relationships in *Hunt for the Wilderpeople*.

Include quotations from the film to support your ideas.

Your essay should include an introduction and a conclusion. Organize the main body of your essay using PEA paragraphs.

You have 60 minutes to complete the task.

Reflection

In this chapter we have watched Taika Waititi's *Hunt for the Wilderpeople* and have explored how film can be used to engage **audiences** and raise awareness about important social issues. Through the relationships between the **characters** of Hec and Ricky we have learned that making **connections** with others can help to heal the pain and trauma that come with loss and abandonment, key **themes** which are explored in the film.

Use this table to reflect on your own learning in this chapter.					
Questions we asked	Answers we found	Any further questions now?			
Factual: What is whānau? What is foster care?					
Conceptual: How can film help us to understand other cultures? How can films be used to critique social injustice? Why should we express our feelings? Why do we need to belong? What can we gain from our relationships with others? How can we cope with loss?					
Debatable: How can we tackle social inequality? Does the media glamourize gang culture?					
Approaches to learning you used in this chapter:	Description – what new skills did you learn?	How well did you master the skills?			
		Novice	Learner	Practitioner	Expert
Communication skills					
Collaboration skills					
Thinking skills					
Research skills					
Critical-thinking skills					
Affective skills					
Organization skills					
Learner profile attribute(s)	Reflect on the importance of caring for your learning in this chapter.				
Caring					

| Perspective | Character; Context; Setting; Theme | Fairness and Development |

4 Should we forgive and forget?

○ Despite its 400-year-old **context**, through exploring **character, setting and theme** in *The Tempest*, we can develop new and challenge existing **perspectives** on what is **fair** and what is not.

CONSIDER AND ANSWER THESE QUESTIONS:

Factual: What is a 'tempest'? What is 'colonialism'?

Conceptual: Why should we read *The Tempest*? How does Shakespeare establish setting? What lessons can we learn about forgiveness in the play? What can we learn about contemporary beliefs regarding magic from the play?

Debatable: Is *The Tempest* a play about colonialism? How easy is it to distinguish men from monsters? Is it always better to forgive and forget?

Now **share and compare** your thoughts and ideas with your partner, or with the whole class

○ IN THIS CHAPTER, WE WILL …

- **Find out** what a tempest is and learn about some of the contextual factors surrounding the play.
- **Explore** how we can use *The Tempest* to explore issues such as colonialism, injustice and forgiveness.
- **Take action** to help raise awareness about modern slavery.

KEY WORDS

tempest
cartography
colonialism
decolonization
prose
verse
magus
occult

■ These Approaches to Learning (ATL) skills will be useful …

- Thinking skills
- Communication skills
- Research skills
- Collaborative skills

● We will reflect on this learner profile attribute …

- Principled – We act with integrity and honesty, with a strong sense of fairness and justice, and with respect for the dignity and rights of people everywhere.

◆ Assessment opportunities in this chapter:

- Criterion A: Analysing
- Criterion B: Organizing
- Criterion C: Producing text
- Criterion D: Using language

ACTIVITY: What is a tempest?

■ ATL

- Information literacy skills: Access information to be informed and inform others
- Creative-thinking skills: Create original works and ideas

Look at the images above. Discuss the subject of the images and what feelings they evoke.

Use an online dictionary to define the word 'tempest'.

Use the images to write a short description of what you see and **reflect** on how you might feel if you were experiencing first-hand what is depicted in the paintings.

Keep this description as you will be referring to it later on in this chapter.

◆ Assessment opportunities

- In this activity you have practised skills that are assessed using Criterion C: Producing text and Criterion D: Using language.

4 Should we forgive and forget?

Why should we read *The Tempest*?

Described by Samuel Taylor Coleridge as 'a birth of the imagination', *The Tempest* is widely believed to be the last play written by William Shakespeare. A tale of intrigue and magic, the play has introduced audiences to some of the most memorable characters and lines in the history of English drama and remains one of the Bard's most popular plays.

But why should we be interested in a play written in 1611? What relevance could it still have to our lives today? Well, *The Tempest*, like many of Shakespeare's other plays, contains valuable lessons from which we as modern readers and audiences can benefit. Despite the seventeenth-century context and fantastical elements, the play abounds with relevant messages about forgiveness and justice and teaches us to challenge the ways in which we see others and the world around us.

▼ Links to: Mathematics

Act V? Scene IV? Chapter X? Year MCMXCIX? What on earth does it all mean? As a student of Language and Literature you will often be confronted with Roman numerals, which is the representation of numbers using certain letters.

Use the following key to help you work out numbers when they appear in this form.

I = 1
V = 5
X = 10
L = 50
C = 100
D = 500
M = 1000

So, to work out what Chapter XIII is, you need to do some simple addition:

X + I + I + I = 10 + 1 + 1 + 1 = 13

To work out what Scene IV is, you need to do some simple subtraction:

V − I = 5 − 1 = 4

Tip: For bigger numbers, split up the numerals into smaller denominations.

Why not have a go at writing your year of birth in Roman numerals?

Language & Literature for the IB MYP 2: *by Concept*

ACTIVITY: Understanding the plot

■ **ATL**

■ Communication skills: Make effective summary notes for studying

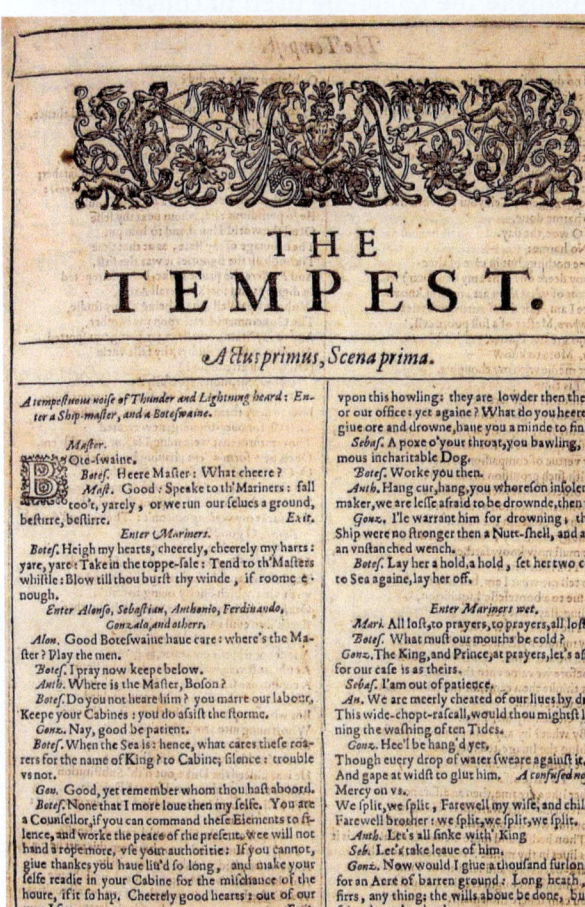

Reading a whole play by Shakespeare from beginning to end in the original language can be tough work, so it might be useful to listen to a brief synopsis, or summary, before we explore the text in further detail.

Visit the link below and watch the video.

www.rsc.org.uk/the-tempest/the-plot

As you watch, make notes about what happens in the play. Use the following questions to help you with your note-taking.

Think carefully about how you will organize your notes so they can be used later to help you access the content of the play.

Now, in pairs or groups:

1 Create a mind map of everything **you already know** about *The Tempest* and Shakespeare.
2 Write down some questions about what **you would like to know** about *The Tempest* (the plot, the characters, the context). We will review these questions later on.

◆ **Assessment opportunities**

◆ In this activity you have practised skills that are assessed using Criterion B: Organizing.

4 Should we forgive and forget? 81

How does Shakespeare establish setting?

WHERE IS PROSPERO'S ISLE?

■ Walter Raleigh's Virginia

The action of the play takes place almost entirely on an island, the exact location of which remains unspecified. But, as King Alonso and his party are travelling from Tunis to Naples at the start of the play, we can deduce that the island is somewhere in the Mediterranean Sea. However, the play does contain some references to the Caribbean which throws the original theory into doubt!

In the early-seventeenth century, the first English colonies were established in Virginia, North America, so it is quite likely that Shakespeare would have encountered contemporary written accounts of voyages to 'The New World' (The Americas, Canada and Mexico). William Strachey's *A true repertory of the wracke* from 1610 is thought to have been one of the sources which may have inspired *The Tempest*. The manuscript consists of a dramatic account of Strachey's experience of a 'most dreadfull Tempest' and subsequent shipwreck on the Bermudas.

Shakespeare's decision to set his play on an isolated island, removed from all civilization, gives him free reign to make it as magical as he pleases, and in this section we will explore the language and stylistic choices he employs to transport us to Prospero's Isle.

ACTIVITY: Setting the scene: Act I

■ **ATL**

■ Communication skills: Read critically and for comprehension

Read Act I, Scene I of the play and complete the following tasks:

1 **Outline** what occurs in the opening scene of the play.
2 **Identify** examples of language in the text which create a sense of action in the scene.
3 **Interpret** how the characters in the scene feel about their situation. **Justify** your response using evidence from the text.
4 **Analyse** the language used to convey the storm. Can you **identify** any stylistic choices Shakespeare has made for this purpose?
5 **Analyse** the lines *'What cares these roarers/ for the name of king?'* What point is being made about power here?
6 **Examine** and **discuss** the importance of the storm in the play. As you discuss, consider the title of the play.
7 How is the tempest described in this scene? Consider the language used by the characters and the stage directions. Look back at the description of a storm you wrote at the beginning of this chapter and **compare and contrast** it with the description of the tempest in Act I, Scene I of the play.

◆ Assessment opportunities

◆ In this activity you have practised skills that are assessed using Criterion A: Analysing.

Hint

Still finding it hard to make head or tail of Shakespeare? Well have no fear!

No Fear Shakespeare is a wonderful online resource where the original texts of Shakespeare's plays are placed alongside a modern version.

You can find the modern version of *The Tempest* by following the link: https://www.sparknotes.com/nofear/shakespeare/tempest/

ACTIVITY: *Dramatis personae* – who's who in *The Tempest*?

ATL

- Communication skills: Make inferences and draw conclusions

ALONSO, king of Naples.
SEBASTIAN, his brother.
PROSPERO, the right duke of Milan.
ANTONIO, his brother, the usurping duke of Milan.
FERDINAND, son to the king of Naples.
GONZALO, an honest old Counsellor.
ADRIAN & FRANCISCO, Lords.
CALIBAN, a savage and deformed Slave.
TRINCULO, a Jester.
STEPHANO, a drunken Butler.
Master of a Ship.
Boatswain.
Mariners.
MIRANDA, daughter to Prospero.
ARIEL, an airy Spirit.
IRIS, CERES, JUNO, Nymphs, Reapers: Spirits.

■ Miranda and Prospero are two of the main characters in Shakespeare's *The Tempest*

The **dramatis personae** of a work of drama is a list of characters that feature in the play. In the Early Modern Period (the name we give the period during which Shakespeare lived and wrote) it was common practice to list the names hierarchically; this could mean in terms of social status, prominence in the play or gender. In pairs look at the list opposite and complete the tasks which follow.

1. What inferences can you make about attitudes held by Shakespeare's contemporaries about social class and the position of men and women at the time the play was written and performed?
2. Which characters have you encountered already? What have you learned about them?
3. As we read the play you will learn more and more about the characters. For each of the highlighted characters in the list (Trinculo and Stephano can be included together) use the template below to **create** a resource which you can use to record information and key quotations. What learner profile attributes does each character possess? Which do they lack?

Character: NAME			
Learner profile attribute	Notes	Evidence (key quotations)	Reference: Act? Scene? Line number? Page number?
Inquirers			
Knowledgeable			
Thinkers			
Communicators			
Principled			
Open-minded			
Caring			
Risk-takers			
Balanced			
Reflective			

◆ Assessment opportunities

♦ In this activity you have practised skills that are assessed using Criterion B: Organizing.

4 Should we forgive and forget?

ACTIVITY: 'Hell is empty, And all the devils are here!'

ATL

- Communication skills: Read critically and for comprehension

As a class, act out Act I, Scene II and complete the tasks which follow:

Task 1: Initial questions

1 Which new characters are you introduced to in this scene? Consider the characters who play a part in this scene rather than those who are only mentioned.
2 What do you learn about the cause of the tempest which takes place in the previous scene?
3 **Identify** Miranda's age in this scene. **Use** evidence from the text to support your answer.
4 Who in the scene has the most lines? **Interpret** what this might mean in terms of power in the play.
5 What more do we learn about the setting of the play?
6 **Identify** and **analyse** the simile Ariel uses to convey a sense of Ferdinand's fear.
7 Using a few sentences **summarize** the key events which take place in this scene.
8 What do you learn about Prospero's relationship with Ariel and Caliban?

Task 2

You and a partner will be allocated a character from the scene. For your character, complete the following tasks. You will have to share your information with others so consider carefully how you will record and present your work.

1 Write down *everything* you learn about your character. What is their story? What do you learn about their past experiences? Their relationships? Their personality?
2 **Explore** your character's lines in the play and **select** some key quotations which you think reveal something about their personality.
3 Annotate these quotations in detail. **Analyse** the use and effect of language and stylistic choices.
4 Draw an image of how you imagine they would look.
5 Think of an object or symbol which you think best reflects your character and use it to **create** a simile to **justify** your choice. (Miranda is a like a … because she …)

Task 3

Join with another pair and share what you have learned. Repeat this until you have covered all of the characters in the scene between you.

As you learn about each character, you might want to use this as an opportunity to start filling in the learner profile table you created earlier.

◆ Assessment opportunities

- In this activity you have practised skills that are assessed using Criterion A: Analysing and Criterion D: Using language.

ACTIVITY: The island

ATL

- Communication skills: Read critically and for comprehension

In Act II, Scene I, the play's focus shifts to some of the other survivors of the shipwreck. As they make sense of the tragedy which has befallen them, Gonzalo and Adrian try to raise spirits by describing the positive aspects of the island.

In pairs read the scene and complete the following tasks:

1 **Identify** the qualities of the island described by Adrian and Gonzalo.
2 Do the others share their point of view? **Justify** your answer with evidence from the text.
3 Write a paragraph explaining what this reveals about perspective.

EXTENSION
Shakespeare's contemporaries

- Miguel Cervantes, widely regarded as the greatest writer in the Spanish language, was writing during Shakespeare's time.

Shakespeare's writing may have captured the imagination of British audiences during his time, but he wasn't the only talented writer out there.

Use the internet to carry out some research about **sixteenth and seventeenth century writers** from your home country.

Find out …

- Where and when they lived.
- The major works they produced.
- The key themes or issues explored in their work.
- Other interesting facts or details about them.

4 Update the table you created earlier for these new characters.
5 What do Sebastian and Antonio plot to do in this scene? How and why does Ariel intervene?

◆ Assessment opportunities

- In this activity you have practised skills that are assessed using Criterion A: Analysing and Criterion D: Using language.

ACTIVITY: Travel writing

ATL

- Creative-thinking skills: Create original works and ideas

- *Miranda – The Tempest*, John William Waterhouse, 1917

During the Age of Discovery, travel wasn't a possibility for the majority of people so to get a taste of the exotic, one had to rely on reading travel narratives.

Make a list of what you think an effective piece of travel writing should include. If you need inspiration, visit the following link for some tips:

www.theguardian.com/travel/2011/sep/23/travel-writing-tips-expert-advice

Imagine yourself in the shoes of one of the shipwrecked characters you have encountered.

Create a piece of travel writing recording your first impressions of the island. Enrich your piece by including quotations from the play.

◆ Assessment opportunities

- In this activity you have practised skills that are assessed using Criterion B: Organizing, Criterion C: Producing text and Criterion D: Using language.

How easy is it to distinguish men from monsters?

IS THE TEMPEST A PLAY ABOUT COLONIALISM?

The late-sixteenth century saw the beginnings of the British Empire; the British began to establish overseas colonies during the reign of Elizabeth I, and when Shakespeare was writing *The Tempest*, England was engaged in the colonization of Ireland. It is therefore almost impossible to read the play without exploring it within the context of colonialism. Use the internet to find a **definition of colonialism**.

The Tempest can be used to explore the complex and problematic relationships between the European colonizers and the colonized indigenous inhabitants of the seized land. In the play, the role of colonizer is played by Prospero, despite his presence on the island being due to misfortune rather than intention, and the roles of the colonized are taken on by Caliban and Ariel.

The play also explores the fears and opportunities that are created by colonization. We see prejudices surrounding race which come to light when people are confronted with difference and how new places can inspire hope for the future. Most worrying is the corrupting influence of power and how it can lead to the commodification and enslavement of others.

By placing these two groups of people in opposition, the supposedly civilized Europeans juxtaposed with the supposedly barbarous natives, Shakespeare invites us to question who the real monsters actually are.

■ Elizabeth I shows us who's boss in what is known as the 'Ditchley Portrait'. She stands with her feet firmly planted on the globe.

Links to: Individuals and Society/Geography – cartography

Maps became more advanced during the sixteenth and seventeenth centuries

Cartography is the science or practice of drawing maps. Humans have made maps for thousands of years but it was during the Age of Exploration, in the sixteenth and seventeenth centuries, that dramatic advancements were made in cartography.

But maps are more than just a means of finding your way from A to B. Not only can we learn a great deal about the past from looking at maps from bygone eras, but we can use modern mapping technology to really make a difference in our world today.

Visit the links below to learn more about the history of cartography and to find out why maps matter:

www.youtube.com/watch?v=fLdvInDrQ2c

https://vimeo.com/54050157

ACTIVITY: Of the Caniballes

ATL

- Critical-thinking skills: Draw reasonable conclusions and generalizations

A picture from 1586 presents the indigenous people, plants and animals of Brazil. What impact might this image have had on an audience at the time? What perceptions might they have formed about the New World?

During the late-sixteenth and early-seventeenth centuries, European explorers took to the seas and ventured out to seek 'new' lands. These voyages of discovery inspired art, literature, cartography and philosophical thought.

The French philosopher Michel de Montaigne penned his essay *Of the Caniballes* after hearing reports into the exploration of Brazil.

You can read an extract from it here:

> Now, to return to my subject, I find that there is nothing barbarous and savage in this nation, by anything that I can gather, excepting, that every one gives the title of barbarism to everything that is not in use in his own country. As, indeed, we have no other level of truth and reason than the example and idea of the opinions and customs of the place wherein we live: there is always the perfect religion, there the perfect government, there the most exact and accomplished usage of all things.

In pairs, discuss the following:

1. What point does Montaigne make about the native population in the land he is describing? Which IB learner profile attribute does this suggest Montaigne possesses? Explain why.
2. What does Montaigne suggest about our perspectives on ourselves and others? What is your opinion of this?
3. Which of the characters you have encountered so far in *The Tempest* appears to have the same mindset and way of thinking as Montaigne? Use evidence from the play to **justify** your response.

◆ Assessment opportunities

- In this activity you have practised skills that are assessed using Criterion A: Analysing.

ACTIVITY: Act II, Scene II – men or monsters?

ATL

- Communication skills: Read critically and for comprehension; Make inferences and draw conclusions
- Critical-thinking skills: Evaluate evidence or argument

1. Read Act II, Scene II of the play and summarize what takes place.
2. Read Trinculo's lines below and complete the tasks:

What do we learn about Caliban's appearance?

What opportunities does Caliban present to Trinculo?

Trinculo: What have we here? A man or a fish? Dead or alive? A fish. He smells like a fish, a very ancient and fish-like smell, a kind of not-of-the-newest poor-john. A strange fish! Were I in England now, as once I was, and had but this fish painted, not a holiday fool there but would give a piece of silver. There would this monster make a man. Any strange beast there makes a man. When they will not give a doit to relieve a lame beggar, they will lay out ten to see a dead Indian. Legged like a man and his fins like arms! Warm, o' my troth. I do now let loose my opinion, hold it no longer: this is no fish, but an islander that hath lately suffered by a thunderbolt.

Analyse the language Trinculo uses to talk about Caliban. What might this reveal about contemporary attitudes towards people from other places and cultures?

3. **Analyse** Stephano's lines in this scene and **explore** how Shakespeare tackles power and the commodification of people.
4. Both men speak about Caliban in a derogatory manner, referring to him as a 'monster'. In pairs, **evaluate** who behaves more monstrously in this scene. **Justify** your answers using evidence from the text.

Assessment opportunities

- In this activity you have practised skills that are assessed using Criterion A: Analysing.

Look at the way Trinculo's lines are **organized** on the page. Do you notice any differences between this and some of the lines spoken by other characters in the play? Why do you think this is?

Verse or prose?

Trinculo's lines differ from those spoken by characters like Prospero, because they are delivered in **prose** rather than **verse**. But, what is the difference between prose and verse and why does Shakespeare switch between the two?

Prose is writing that follows the standard rules of grammar and appears a certain way on the page. **Verse**, however, refers to a type of writing which is arranged in a **rhythm** and typically has a **rhyme**. Poems are an example of texts which are written in verse.

Shakespeare's plays contain both prose and verse; you can tell when a character is speaking in prose because on the page the text will reach the margin, whereas when a character speaks in verse, the text will be arranged in a narrower block, to the left of the page, with each new line beginning with a capital letter.

When Shakespeare chooses to make a character speak in prose or poetry, he is doing so in order to reveal something about that character. Comic or low status characters often speak in prose, whilst verse is deemed more suitable for the more important characters, or those of higher social status.

Trinculo and Stephano both speak in prose. Infer what this reveals about their positions within the play.

ACTIVITY: Can you empathize with a character like Caliban?

■ **ATL**

■ Communication skills: Make inferences and draw conclusions

Described by Prospero as a 'poisonous slave', 'a freckled whelp' who is 'not honour'd with a human shape', Caliban has divided audiences for decades.

Should we dislike him for being the villain he seems to be or does he deserve our sympathy?

To begin, look at the images below. In pairs **discuss** the following:

- How is Caliban presented in each of these images? What does he look like?
- In the images where he is with other characters from the play, what kind of position does he occupy?
- **Evaluate** the images and decide which one corresponds most with what you have read about Caliban so far. **Justify** your answer using quotations from the text.
- What does this reveal about attitudes towards 'outsiders' during Shakespeare's time?

◆ Assessment opportunities

◆ In this activity you have practised skills that are assessed using Criterion A: Analysing.

4 Should we forgive and forget?

ACTIVITY: *Une Tempête* – postcolonial re-imaginings of *The Tempest*

■ **ATL**

■ Communication skills: Make inferences and draw conclusions

Decolonization is the process by which colonised countries gain independence from their colonizers. In particular, the term has come to refer to the dismantling of colonial empires following the Second World War. This was a global phenomenon, but decolonization movements in Africa, the Caribbean, and Latin America gained momentum in the 1960s and 70s.

Many opponents of colonial rule in their countries felt that the colonizers were attempting to erase indigenous customs, traditions and languages and replace them with their own. According to Kenyan writer, Ngũgĩ wa Thiong'o, *'The bullet was the means of physical subjugation. Language was the means of the spiritual subjugation.'*

In pairs, complete the following tasks:
- **Interpret** what the quotation means. Do you agree or disagree with the argument?
- **Discuss** how you can link this idea to *The Tempest*. How is the theme of language explored in the play? Use evidence from the text to support your ideas.

■ Césaire wrote a version of *The Tempest* (*Une Tempête*) in 1969

Aimé Césaire, a writer and activist from Martinique, wrote *Une Tempête* in 1969. Césaire sets his play in a colony, where characters such as Caliban defiantly resist colonial subjugation.

Read the extracts from *Une Tempête* and compare and contrast Césaire's presentation of the characters of Caliban and Prospero to Shakespeare's in Act I, Scene II of *The Tempest*.

Organize your response using two comparative PEA paragraphs. Comment on the writers' use of language and stylistic choices.

Can you link your ideas back to Ngũgĩ wa Thiong'o's quotation about language?

■ *'The bullet was the means of physical subjugation. Language was the means of the spiritual subjugation.'*
Ngũgĩ wa Thiong'o

Prospero: Since you're so fond of invective, you could at least thank me for having taught you to speak at all. You, a savage… a dumb animal, you beast I educated, trained, dragged up from the bestiality that still clings to you.

Caliban: In the first place, that's not true. You didn't teach me a thing! Except to jabber in your own language that I could understand your orders: chop the wood, wash the dishes, fish for food, plant vegetables, all because you're too lazy to do it yourself. And as for your learning, did you ever impart any of that to me? No, you took care not to. All your science you keep for yourself alone, shut up in those big books.

Caliban: It's this: I've decided I don't want to be called Caliban any longer.

Prospero: What kind of rot is that? I don't understand.

Caliban: Put it this way: I'm telling you that from now on I won't answer to the name Caliban.

Prospero: Where did you get that idea?

Caliban: Well, because Caliban isn't my name. It's as simple as that.

Prospero: Oh, I suppose it's mine!

Caliban: It's the name given to me by your hatred, and every time it's spoken it's an insult.

Prospero: My, aren't we getting sensitive! All right, suggest something else… I've got to call you something. What will it be? Cannibal would suit you, but I'm sure you wouldn't like that, would you? Let's see… what about Hannibal? That fits. And why not… they all seem to like historical names.

Caliban: Call me X. That would be best. Like a man without a name. Or to be more precise, a man whose name has been stolen. You talk about history… well, that's history, and everyone knows it! Every time you summon me it reminds me of a basic fact, the fact that you've stolen everything from me, even my identity! Uhuru! (He exits.)

> Comment on Prospero's use of wordplay. What does it reveal about colonial stereotypes?

ⓘ Did you know …

… that although slavery was abolished in Britain in 1807, Parliament had to create anti-slavery powers in 2009 to prosecute a woman who had been found guilty of trafficking a woman from Tanzania into the UK to work as her domestic slave?

Although the legislation made it easier to convict people for such crimes, slavery cases weren't being dealt with properly, and in 2015, the Modern Slavery Act was passed.

Find out more about modern slavery and how you can help put an end to it by visiting the link below:

www.antislavery.org/slavery-today/modern-slavery/

◆ Assessment opportunities

- In this activity you have practised skills that are assessed using Criterion A: Analysing, Criterion B: Organizing and Criterion D: Using language.

4 Should we forgive and forget?

▼ Links to: Arts – Drama; The log scene; Act III, Scene I

Plays are written to be performed, so acting out the plays of Shakespeare, or seeing them acted out, can help us understand the work in greater depth.

Although Shakespeare includes stage directions in his play, it is sometimes difficult to know how exactly he would have wanted his characters to deliver their lines.

It is up to the director and the actors to interpret the play as they see fit, and these interpretations often reflect the ideas and values of the audiences for which they are being performed.

Visit the link and listen to actors Jenny Rainsford and Daniel Easton talk about Miranda and Ferdinand, the characters they played in the Royal Shakespeare Company's 2016 production of *The Tempest*.

www.youtube.com/watch?v=ml0PdATMDDw

- Why do you think it is important for them as actors to understand the characters, their desires and motivations?
- What points do they make about the way in which the two characters speak?
- **Critique** the different ways in which the scene is played out. **Evaluate** which is the most effective. Which version do you think is closest to what Shakespeare intended?
- Consider the stage imagery and costumes in the live production. How do they help to set the scene?
- What impact does including humour in the scene have on the audience? Analyse the way traditional sixteenth- and seventeenth-century gender roles are subverted by the actors to cater for the modern audience.

ACTIVITY: Act III, Scene II – Prospero's books

■ **ATL**

- Communication skills: Make inferences and draw conclusions

Read Act III, Scene II and complete the tasks:

1 **Summarize** what takes place in this scene.
2 **Comment** on Caliban's relationship with the two men.
3 What do the men plot to do and why?
4 Why does Caliban want to destroy Prospero's books? **Interpret** what they symbolize in the play.
5 Discuss whether you think Caliban would be in a better position if his plan were to succeed. Explain why. How does this make you feel towards Caliban?
6 Look closely at Caliban's lines from 'Be not afeard' to 'I cried to dream again.' **Identify** and **analyse** his use of language and stylistic choices. Does he speak in prose or verse?
7 **Compare and contrast** these lines to some of the other lines he speaks in the play.
8 In pairs **discuss** what these lines reveal to us about his character.

So far in this chapter we have explored Shakespeare's use of character and setting and used this to develop an understanding of some of the contextual factors surrounding *The Tempest*. We have carried out some close literary analysis of language and stylistic choices in the play and have considered the play as an early literary exploration of colonialism.

What can we learn about contemporary beliefs regarding magic from the play?

■ James VI, King of Scotland (later James I of England), was convinced that a coven of witches was conspiring to murder him through magic. The accused confessed after being subjected to torture.

Shakespeare lived in a society where a belief in the supernatural was not only common, but was so deeply entrenched that this was even reflected in the country's laws! Certain Acts prescribed heavy penalties for the practice of sorcery or witchcraft, and many hundreds of men and women were executed for 'crimes' of this nature.

John Dee, a scholar, astrologer and magician, was a prominent figure during the Tudor period and was accused of sorcery many times during his lifetime. A trusted advisor to Elizabeth I, who was deeply superstitious herself (it was said that she gave the Earl of Essex a magic ring to protect him on his travels), Dee had a reputation as a magus, or mage, a sorcerer who has acquired his knowledge of the occult through extensive study. Unfortunately for Dee, not all monarchs gave him the same respect as Elizabeth; he was imprisoned in 1555 by Mary and later accused of sorcery by Elizabeth's successor, James I.

Dee had one of the largest private libraries in England at the time, and like Prospero prized his books dearly. In fact, Dee could well have been the inspiration for Shakespeare's Prospero. You can visit the link to find out more: **https://history.rcplondon.ac.uk/blog/rapt-secret-studies-was-shakespeares-prospero-inspired-john-dee**

■ The scholar, astrologer and magician John Dee (left) is often seen as a model for Shakespeare's Prospero.

EXTENSION

Can belief in magic be dangerous?

■ ATL

- Collaboration skills: Listen actively to other perspectives and ideas
- Information literacy skills: Access information to be informed and inform others

In pairs, **discuss** the following:

1 Do you believe in magic? Are you superstitious? What attitudes towards magic, witchcraft and sorcery are held in your country or culture?

2 Why do you think people in Shakespeare's time believed in sorcery and witchcraft? What does this reveal about society at that time?

3 **Evaluate** whether Prospero uses his magic responsibly. Justify your answer with reference to the text.

4 Can a belief in magic be dangerous? Explain why.

5 **Use** the internet to find out about the **dangers of superstitious beliefs in the modern world**. You can start by reading the following article: https://bbc.in/3bUylx2

ACTIVITY: The banquet scene

■ **ATL**

- Critical-thinking skills: Draw reasonable conclusions and generalizations
- Media literacy skills: Demonstrate an awareness of media interpretation of events and ideas

■ *I cannot too much muse*
Such shapes, such gesture, and such sound, expressing,
Although they want the use of tongue, a kind
Of excellent dumb discourse. Alonso, Act III, Scene III

■ *Ariel*, a painting by the Swiss painter, Henry Fuseli

Visit the link and watch Act III, Scene III from director Julie Taymor's 2010 film version of *The Tempest* and complete the tasks.

www.youtube.com/watch?v=lxKC9TPnwTM

1 **Summarize** how Prospero uses his magic in this scene.
2 What does this use of magic reveal to us about the character of Prospero and his ideas about justice?
3 What does Gonzalo say to reassure the other men? What does this reveal about how contemporary ideas about foreign lands and people were shaped?
4 What do you notice about Taymor's Prospero in this interpretation? **Discuss** why she might have made this choice.
5 In the play the stage directions state that 'ARIEL enters in the form of a harpy; ARIEL flaps his wings on the table, and the banquet vanishes from the table'. **Analyse** the presentation of Ariel in this scene. What kind of atmosphere is created and how?
6 What does Ariel tell the men? Explain the impact this revelation has on them.
7 Refer back to Act I, Scene II of the play. What do you learn about Caliban's mother, Sycorax? What is the difference between her magic and Prospero's 'art'?

■ In Greek and Roman mythology, a harpy was a monstrous **personification** of storm winds. A harpy is often depicted as having a woman's head and body and a bird's wings and claws.

◆ Assessment opportunities

♦ In this activity you have practised skills that are assessed using Criterion A: Analysing, Criterion B: Organizing and Criterion D: Using language.

Did you know …

… *The Tempest* was one of 14 plays which were performed as part of the elaborate festivities in honour of the betrothal and marriage of King James I's 16-year-old daughter, Princess Elizabeth Stuart, to Frederick V, heir to the German Palatinate? The wedding took place on 14 February 1613 in the royal chapel at Whitehall Palace and was a grand affair; **masques** were performed and Elizabeth, covered in valuable jewels, wore a dress made of silver cloth and taffeta, and needed 16 bridesmaids to carry her train.

ACTIVITY: 'Our revels now are ended'

ATL

- Communication skills: Read critically and for comprehension

In Act IV, Scene I of the play, Prospero finally gives his approval to the relationship between Ferdinand and Miranda, and to celebrate their union, summons Ariel and three other spirits to perform a masque for the young couple:

> *What are the connotations of this word?*
>
> Go bring the rabble,
> O'er whom I give thee power, here to this place.
> Incite them to quick motion, for I must
> Bestow upon the eyes of this young couple
> Some vanity of mine art. It is my promise,
> And they expect it from me.

What do these words suggest about how Prospero, or indeed Shakespeare, perceives himself and his 'art'?

Read the remainder of the scene as a class and then complete the following tasks:

1 **Identify** the reason Prospero suddenly ends the performance.
2 Visit the link below and watch actor David Threlfall's performance of Prospero's speech to Ferdinand. **Interpret** what he means when he speaks the lines 'We are such stuff / As dreams are made on, and our little life / Is rounded with a sleep.' What point is Prospero making about life? www.theguardian.com/stage/video/2016/feb/29/david-threlfall-prospero-the-tempest-our-revels-now-are-ended-shakespeare-video
3 **Summarize** how Prospero deals with Caliban, Stephano and Trinculo in the latter half of this scene.

- 'Seest thou here, This is the mouth o' th' cell. No noise, and enter. Do that good mischief which may make this island Thine own for ever, and I, thy Caliban, For aye thy foot-licker.'
Act IV, Scene I

◆ Assessment opportunities

◆ In this activity you have practised skills that are assessed using Criterion A: Analysing.

What lessons can we learn about forgiveness in the play?

IS IT ALWAYS BETTER TO FORGIVE AND FORGET?

Mohandas Gandhi, leader of the Indian Independence movement against British rule, said that 'the weak can never forgive. Forgiveness is the attribute of the strong.' For many scholars, the theme of forgiveness lies at the heart of *The Tempest*, but in the play Prospero is able to pardon the sins of his countrymen only after executing an elaborate and, at times, cruel plan of revenge.

Perhaps there is, as some critics suggest, an absence of true forgiveness in the play, but as modern readers we can still learn a great deal about the futility of vengeance and the peace of mind forgiveness can bring.

> ### THINK–PAIR–SHARE
>
> #### ■ ATL
>
> - Collaboration skills: Listen actively to other perspectives and ideas
> - Information literacy skills: Access information to be informed and inform others
>
> At the end of Act IV, Scene I, Prospero stops the masque he has put on for Ferdinand and Miranda to turn his mind to foiling Caliban's plot. 'I will plague them all, / Even to roaring' he declares.
>
> On your own, copy out and annotate the quotation above and then write your own definition of revenge.
>
> Get into a pair and share your **annotations** and definitions.
>
> - Discuss Prospero's words and share your ideas about the concept of revenge.
> - Have you ever sought revenge?
> - If so, why and under what circumstances?
> - Was your plan of vengeance successful? If so, reflect on how you felt afterwards. Was it indeed, sweet? Explain why or why not.
> - Which characters want revenge in the play and why?
>
> Together, use the internet to find some **idioms** about **revenge** or **vengeance**. **Interpret** and **discuss** what each one means.

ACTIVITY: Is revenge really sweet?

■ ATL

- Critical-thinking skills: Evaluate evidence or argument; Gather and organize relevant information to formulate an argument
- Communication skills: Read critically and for comprehension

Before reading Act V, Scene I, discuss the following questions:

- Is Prospero a naturally forgiving person? What does he want from those who have wronged him before he can offer them forgiveness?
- In your opinion, what is Prospero's greatest cruelty towards Alonso in the play? Does his reason for revenge justify his actions?

Now, read Act V, Scene I and complete the following tasks:

1 Why is this scene significant for Ariel?
2 Look closely at Ariel's lines from 'Confined together' to 'Mine would, sir, were I human.' **Analyse** the language and consider Ariel's influence on Prospero.
3 **Identify** what Prospero pledges to do in his soliloquy. Discuss why he decides to do so.
4 **Evaluate** the reactions of the men to Prospero's revelations. How remorseful are they? Do they genuinely regret their actions?
5 In pairs **discuss** how sincere you believe Prospero's forgiveness to be, focusing especially on the words he addresses to his brother, Antonio. **Analyse** the language and stylistic choices he uses and use them to justify your arguments.
6 What do Miranda and Ferdinand, the younger generation, represent in the play?
7 **Comment** on the relationship between Caliban and Prospero and link it to the themes of forgiveness and revenge.
8 What lessons can we learn about forgiveness and revenge from *The Tempest*?

■ What do Miranda and Ferdinand, the younger generation, represent in the play?

Epilogue

The Tempest ends with an **epilogue**, which is a section of a book or, as in this case, a speech at the end of a play that serves as a comment on or a conclusion to what has occurred in the story.

Some books or plays begin with a **prologue**, which is a separate section which acts as an introduction to the literary or dramatic work.

In *The Tempest*, the epilogue consists of Prospero's final speech. Read it and identify who he is addressing in his final speech and comment on the effect.

ACTIVITY: Comedy, romance or tragedy? Categorising *The Tempest*

■ ATL

- Collaboration skills: Listen actively to other perspectives and ideas
- Critical-thinking skills: Evaluate evidence or argument; Draw reasonable conclusions and generalizations

1 In pairs, read the quotation by the Romantic poet and literary critic Samuel Taylor Coleridge, and discuss what it means. Use an online dictionary to define the words you don't understand:

   The Tempest is a specimen of the purely romantic drama, in which the interest is not historical, or dependent upon fidelity of portraiture, or the natural connexion of events – but is a birth of the imagination.

2 Use a search engine to find out what the conventions of the following genres are:
   o tragedy
   o comedy
   o romance.

3 What conventions of each genre can you identify in *The Tempest*? Do the conventions of any one genre dominate the play?
   Copy and complete the table below, giving yourself enough space to record the relevant information:

Genre	Convention/s	Evidence (quotation / stage direction)
Comedy		
Tragedy		
Romance		

4 In pairs or groups, **evaluate** the content of your tables and **outline** which genre you think *The Tempest* belongs to. Make sure you **justify** your argument with the evidence you have collected.

◆ Assessment opportunities

♦ In this activity you have practised skills that are assessed using Criterion B: Organizing.

4 Should we forgive and forget?

> **! Take action**
>
> **How can I make a difference?**
>
> ! **See things from another perspective:** Has the focus on decolonization in this chapter piqued your interest? Read some post-colonial literature. Post-colonial literature is written by people from or with a connection to a place which has a colonial past and seeks to restore the voices of those left voiceless under oppressive colonial regimes. Use the internet to carry out a search for **post-colonial literature**.
>
> ! **Let it go!:** Have you been holding a grudge? Plotting revenge? Even if you can't forget, be the bigger person and just forgive. It'll make you feel a lot better!
>
> ! **Campaign to put an end to modern slavery:** Raise awareness by making posters or doing an assembly about the plight of millions of people who are forced into slavery around the world. With the help of your teachers, you could organize a charity event to raise money for charities dedicated to the cause.
>
> ! **Read more Shakespeare:** You can never have too much Shakespeare in your life. If you enjoyed the magical elements in *The Tempest* you'll enjoy *A Midsummer's Night Dream*.

A SUMMATIVE PROBLEM TO TRY

Use this task to apply and extend your learning in this chapter. This task is designed so that you can evaluate your learning using the Language and Literature criteria.

Task: Essay

Choose one of the two questions:

- *'... the rarer action is / In virtue than in vengeance'*. The Tempest *teaches us that it is better to forgive and forget than to seek revenge.* How far do you agree with this statement?
- *Caliban is 'the bestial man [with] no sense of right and wrong, and therefore sees no difference between good and evil. His state is less guilty'*, therefore, as an audience we should sympathize with him. How far do you agree with this statement?

Write an argumentative essay to support your point of view.

Spend some time planning before you start writing. Use the following guidelines to help structure your response.

- Establish whether you agree or disagree with the statement in your introduction.
- Include relevant quotations from the play to support your ideas.
- Use PEA paragraphs to organize your response.
- Do acknowledge the other side of the argument in your essay to show that you are a well-informed and balanced writer.
- Briefly summarize your argument in your conclusion.

Reflection

In this chapter we have carried out a study of William Shakespeare's *The Tempest* and, through exploring **character** and **setting**, have developed an understanding of the universal **themes** of forgiveness and revenge. In addition we have examined some of the **contexts** surrounding the production of the text and, through close analysis of language and stylistic choices, have considered the play as an early literary exploration of colonialism which has allowed us to develop a **perspective** on what is **fair** and what is not.

Use this table to reflect on your own learning in this chapter						
Questions we asked	Answers we found	Any further questions now?				
Factual: What is a tempest? What is colonialism?						
Conceptual: Why should we read *The Tempest*? How does Shakespeare establish setting? What lessons can we learn about forgiveness in the play? What can we learn about contemporary beliefs regarding magic from the play?						
Debatable: Is *The Tempest* a play about colonialism? How easy is it to distinguish men from monsters? Is it always better to forgive and forget?						
Approaches to learning you used in this chapter:	Description – what new skills did you learn?	How well did you master the skills?				
		Novice	Learner	Practitioner	Expert	
Thinking skills						
Communication skills						
Research skills						
Collaborative skills						
Learner profile attribute(s)	Reflect on the importance of being principled for your learning in this chapter.					
Principled						

Communication | Structure; Point of View; Purpose | Identities and Relationships

5 Friends forever?

○ Often the **purpose** of a text can be to **communicate** a particular **point of view** about an issue the writer feels strongly about. The **structure** of an epistolary text allows a writer to explore **identities and relationships** in a relatable format.

■ Helen Keller (left) with her devoted teacher and friend, Anne Sullivan (right). Keller lost her sight and hearing when she was afflicted with what may have been scarlet fever at the age of 19 months. Find out more about Keller and Sullivan's friendship by searching online.

CONSIDER AND ANSWER THESE QUESTIONS:

Factual: What is a friendship? What is a novella? What is an epistolary novel or novella? What is anti-Semitism?

Conceptual: Why does friendship matter? What IB learner profile attributes should a good friend possess? What factors can cause a friendship to break down? Can propaganda really change the way we think about the world?

Debatable: Is social media and our increasing use of mobile technology damaging friendships?

Now **share and compare** your thoughts and ideas with your partner, or with the whole class.

○ IN THIS CHAPTER, WE WILL …
- **Find out** what an **epistolary** text is.
- **Explore** how external pressures can break even the strongest of friendships through the study of *Address Unknown*.
- **Take action** to take a stand against prejudice and racial and religious discrimination.

- We will reflect on this learner profile attribute …
  - Open-minded – We critically appreciate our own cultures and personal histories, as well as the values and traditions of others.

- Assessment opportunities in this chapter:
  - Criterion A: Analysing
  - Criterion B: Organizing
  - Criterion C: Producing text
  - Criterion D: Using language

- These Approaches to Learning (ATL) skills will be useful …
  - Communication skills
  - Collaboration skills
  - Research skills
  - Thinking skills
  - Organization skills

KEY WORDS

novella	propaganda
epistolary	anti-Semitism
indoctrination	ideology

THINK–PAIR–SHARE

'Walking with a friend in the dark is better than walking alone in the light.'

Helen Keller

As a class, discuss the quotation above. How far do you agree with Keller? Explain why.

On your own, take a couple of minutes to note down the answers to the following questions:

1. On a scale of one to ten, how important are your friends?
2. How often do you see your friends? How much time per week do you spend with your friends?
3. How many *best* friends do you have? Is it possible to have more than one best friend at a time?
4. Could anything get in the way of your friendship? What?
5. What is the best or most important quality to you in a friend? Why?
6. In your opinion, do you think *all* friendships last forever? Explain with reference to your own personal experiences.
7. Do you have many or any friends that you have known 'forever'? If so, what do you think has made your friendship last?

Get into pairs to discuss your thoughts and feelings about friendship. Be prepared to share your thoughts with the rest of the class.

WHY DOES FRIENDSHIP MATTER?

What would we do without our friends? Friendships are one of life's great pleasures. With our friends we can share our secrets and our sorrows, our deepest fears and our greatest hopes. But even the strongest friendships can crumble under pressure.

Literature often reflects real life and this is why friendship has always been a theme which has attracted writers. The way in which we interact with others can reveal a great deal about ourselves, and through exploring relationships in literature we can develop an understanding of human nature.

In this chapter we will explore the themes of friendship, betrayal and vengeance through studying Kathrine Kressmann Taylor's epistolary **novella**, *Address Unknown*.

5 Friends forever?

What is a novella?

WHAT IS AN EPISTOLARY NOVEL OR NOVELLA?

The term 'epistolary' comes from the word 'epistle' which, put simply, is a form of writing directed to a person or group of people. While this usually means letters, diaries can also fall under this same category.

The roots of the genre lie in the eighteenth century and some of the earliest novels were written in epistolary form. Among these early examples are *Pamela* and *Clarissa*, both written in the 1740s by Samuel Richardson.

As epistolary stories are told in letter or diary form, they are always written in the first person narrative voice. This lends the text a subjectivity, which not only raises questions about the reliability of the narrator, but makes us as readers work harder to figure out what is going on. We must piece together the story from sometimes numerous accounts, all told from different points of view.

■ Samuel Richardson's *Pamela*, one of the earliest novels, was written in epistolary form.

ACTIVITY: *Address Unknown*: Short story, novelette, novella or novel?

■ ATL

■ Information literacy skills: Access information to be informed and inform others

Copy the table. To begin, match the terms to their definitions:

novel   novella   novelette   short story

Term	Definition	Example
	A fictional tale in prose, intermediate in length and complexity between a short story and a novel, and usually concentrating on a single event or chain of events, with a surprising turning point.	
	An invented prose narrative of considerable length and a certain complexity that deals imaginatively with human experience, usually through a connected sequence of events involving a group of persons in a specific setting.	
	Often used derogatorily to describe a work of 'cheap fiction', shorter than a novel but longer than a short story; usually refers to sentimental romances and thrillers of popular appeal but little literary merit.	
	A fictional work of prose that is shorter in length than a novel and which could be read in one sitting. Because of the shorter length, a text of this type usually focuses on one plot, one main character and one central theme.	

In stories told through letters, like Taylor's *Address Unknown*, time is often disrupted and we are required to make inferences about the nature of the relationship between the correspondents and build up a picture of their collective past from clues in the text.

Use the internet to check your answers and find some examples to add to the last column. You can also use examples of literature we have looked at in this book.

Address Unknown has been described as a long short story, a short novel and a novella! It was originally published as a short story in an American magazine in 1938 and then reprinted by *Reader's Digest*. A year later it was published as a book and sold 50 000 copies.

For the purposes of this chapter, and based on the definitions above, we will treat the book as a novella.

◆ Assessment opportunities

♦ In this activity you have practised skills that are assessed using Criterion B: Organizing.

ACTIVITY: *Address Unknown*: Letters one to three

■ ATL

- Communication skills: Read critically and for comprehension
- Information literacy skills: Access information to be informed and inform others

In Taylor's *Address Unknown*, the story unfolds through a series of eighteen letters and one cablegram. Before you begin reading, in pairs discuss what you think the title of the book refers to. What does the phrase mean and where might you find it and why? Keep your ideas in mind or jot them down somewhere. We will return to the title later on.

Read letters one to three of the novella and complete the tasks.

1 **Identify** the two friends this story focuses on and note down any facts you learn about them.
2 What do you notice about the dates of the letters? **Interpret** what this suggests about their relationship.
3 Use clues in the text to **identify** a connection between the two men other than their friendship.
4 What are the 'young sprouts' referred to in the text? What literary device is this?
5 Who is Griselle and what is her relationship with the two men? Find evidence from the text to support your answer.
6 Why has Martin purchased such a large bed for Elsa? Write a short paragraph to explain your answer. Include reference to the text in your response.

◆ Assessment opportunities

♦ In this activity you have practised skills that are assessed using Criterion A: Analysing and Criterion D: Using language.

5 Friends forever?

ACTIVITY: Contexts – research task

ATL

- Communication skills: Make effective summary notes for studying
- Information literacy skills: Access information to be informed and inform others
- Collaboration skills: Exercise leadership and take on a variety of roles within groups; Encourage others to contribute

Address Unknown was published in 1938, a year before the Second World War broke out. Taylor's story of two men, whose friendship deteriorates during Hitler's rise to power in the 1930s, was immediately banned in Germany.

Before we begin to read, it is important that you have some understanding of the context surrounding the novella.

Work in groups and use the internet to carry out research on one of the following topics. Make sure that each member of your group has the same notes. You will be sharing them in a 'carousel' fashion later.

- Group 1: Adolf Hitler and the Nazi Party.
- Group 2: Life in Germany in the 1930s (daily life; education; women; family).
- Group 3: Causes of the Second World War; countries involved; how were the places where you are from affected by the war?
- Group 4: The Holocaust.

You may find the following websites useful:

www.rafmuseum.org.uk

www.iwm.org.uk

https://bit.ly/38WrRvM

https://bit.ly/3qBQT9n

Once you have collected your information, double check that everyone on your table has the same notes and you are in a position to share your knowledge with others.

One person from your group will remain seated at the table. The rest of your group will have to separate and sit at another table. Each new group should be made up of a member from all four groups.

You have the rest of the lesson to share everything you have learned about your topic with the other people in your new group. Make sure the others are making notes as you speak. One of you should take a leadership role to ensure that you all have time to share your information.

◆ Assessment opportunities

- In this activity you have practised skills that are assessed using Criterion B: Organizing and Criterion D: Using language.

Did you know …

… the Hitler Youth were encouraged to burn books that were deemed 'anti-German'? There was a long list of the types of literature that were to be banned, and included:
- the work of anyone who spoke up against the ideals of the new Germany;
- anything that was deemed too decadent and therefore dangerous to the morals of the German people;
- anything that was written by Jews.

The list goes on.

Visit the link to read more about book burning and explore the website further for other resources linked to this topic.

https://www.facinghistory.org/resource-library/where-they-burn-books

The article quotes from an open letter to the Nazi youth written by Helen Keller, who we considered briefly earlier in the chapter.

> Do not imagine that your barbarities to the Jews are unknown here. God sleepeth not, and He will visit His judgment upon you. Better were it for you to have a mill-stone hung around your neck and sink into the sea than to be hated and despised of all men.

You can read the entire letter at
https://www.aph.org/app/uploads/2020/08/HK_Reading3.pdf

■ 'Where they burn books, they will also ultimately burn people.' Heinrich Heine

■ *Self-Portrait as a Soldier* (1915) by German expressionist Ernst Ludwig Kirchner. It wasn't only books that were targeted. Around 600 pieces of his art were destroyed. Kirchner took his own life in 1938.

ACTIVITY: Letter four

ATL

- Communication skills: Read critically and for comprehension
- Critical-thinking skills: Draw reasonable conclusions and generalizations

Look at the date on letter four from Martin to Max. What is its significance? **Compare and contrast** it with the dates on the preceding three letters. Read the letter and complete the tasks.

1. Look at the highlighted words and phrases. **Identify** the linguistic and literary devices.
2. **Analyse** each quotation and comment on the effect.
3. Consider the content of the letter. Can you make any links with the research you carried out on contexts? How does the tone and content differ from his previous letter?
4. How has Martin's language changed? What might have influenced this change?
5. What do you notice about the personal pronouns and determiners he uses? What does this reveal about his identity?
6. **Identify** a quotation which suggests that Martin and others are intimidated by the Nazi regime.
7. What do we learn about Elsa in this letter? Think back to your research and what you found out about women in Nazi Germany.
8. Is any part of the letter still affectionate and friendly?
9. **Evaluate** how sensitive Martin is being when he dismisses pillaging and 'Jewbaiting' as 'minor things'. How might Max feel when he reads about this?
10. In pairs, use what you have read so far to make some predictions about how the men's friendship will be affected by the events in Germany.
11. **Discuss** how you feel after reading this letter. Can epistolary novels create a sense of intimacy that other types of writing cannot?

◆ Assessment opportunities

- In this activity you have practised skills that are assessed using Criterion A: Analysing.

SCHLOSS RANTZENBURG
MUNICH, GERMANY

March 25, 1933

Mr. Max Eisenstein
Schulse-Eisenstein Galleries
San Francisco, California, U.S.A

Dear Old Max:

You have heard of course of the new events in Germany, and you will want to know how it appears to us here on the inside. I tell you truly, Max, I think in many ways Hitler is good for Germany, but I am not sure. He is now the active head of the government. I doubt much that even Hindenburg could now remove him from power, as he was truly forced to place him there. The man is like an electric shock, strong as only a great orator and a zealot can be. But I ask myself, is he quite sane? His brown shirt troops are of the rabble. They pillage and have started a bad Jewbaiting. But these may be minor things, the little surface scum when a big movement boils up. For I tell you, my friend, there is a surge — a surge. The people everywhere have had a quickening. You feel it in the streets and shops. The old despair has been thrown aside like a forgotten coat. No longer the people wrap themselves in shame; they hope again. Perhaps there may be found an end to this poverty. Something, I do not know what, will happen. A leader is found! Yet cautiously to myself I ask, a leader to where? Despair overthrown often turns us in mad directions.

Publicly, as is natural, I express no doubt. I am now an official and a worker in the new regime and I exult very loud indeed. All of us officials who cherish whole skins are quick to join the National Socialists. That is the name for Herr Hitler's party. But also it is not only expedient, there is something more, a feeling that we of Germany have found our destiny and that the future sweeps toward us in an overwhelming wave. We too must move. We must go with it. Even now there are being wrongs done. The storm troopers are having their moment of victory, and there are bloody heads and sad hearts to show for it. But these things pass; if the end in view is right they pass and are forgotten. History writes a clean new page.

All I now ask myself, and I can say to you what I cannot say to any here is: Is the end right? Do we make for a better goal? For you know, Max, I have seen these people of my race since I came here, and I have learned what agonies they have suffered, what years of less and less bread, of leaner bodies, of the end of hope. The quicksand of despair held them, it was at their chins. Then just before they died a man came and pulled them out. All they now know is, they will not die. They are in hysteria of deliverance, almost they worship him. But whoever the savior was, they would have done the same. God grant it is a true leader and no black angel they follow so joyously. To you alone, Max, I say I do not know. I do not know. Yet I hope.

So much for politics. Ourselves, we delight in our new home and have done much entertaining. Tonight the mayor is our guest, at a dinner for twenty-eight. We spread ourselves a little, maybe, but that is to be forgiven. Elsa has a new gown of blue velvet, and is in terror for fear it will not be big enough. She is with child again. There is the way to keep a wife contented, Max. Keep her so busy with babies she has no time to fret.

Our Heinrich has made a social conquest. He goes out on his pony and gets himself thrown off, and who picks him up but the Baron Von Freische. They have a long conversation about America, and one day the baron calls and we have coffee. Heinrich will go there to lunch next week. What a boy! It is too bad his German is not better but he delights everyone.

So we go, my friend, perhaps to become part of great events, perhaps only to pursue our simple family way, but never abandoning that trueness of friendship, of which you speak so movingly. Our hearts go out to you across the wide sea, and when the glasses are filled we toast 'Uncle Max.'

Yours in affectionate regard,

Martin

Pronouns and possessive determiners

Read the passage below and discuss what could be changed to improve your experience of reading it.

Minh and Nosmot went to the National Gallery. Nosmot stopped in front of the Monet painting when Nosmot and Minh got to the gallery. Nosmot asked Minh what Minh thought of the Monet painting.

Re-write the passage using pronouns **they**, **she** and **it**, to replace some of the proper nouns.

Pronouns are words which replace nouns in sentences. Evaluate your new passage. What makes it better to read?

People often confuse possessive determiners with pronouns, particularly the words: **your, my, our, their, her**.

These words cannot be used to replace nouns, but rather appear *before* a noun to determine who owns it, for example **my** car; **her** book; **their** house; **our** country.

Can propaganda really change the way we think about the world?

WHAT FACTORS CAN CAUSE A FRIENDSHIP TO BREAK?

■ *Paul Alexis Reading a Manuscript to Emile Zola*, by Paul Cézanne, c.1870

To Émile Zola

Gardanne, April 4 1886

Mon cher Émile,

I've just received *L'Œuvre*, which you were kind enough to send me. I thank the author of the *Rougon-Macquart* for this kind token of remembrance, and ask him to allow me to wish him well, thinking of years gone by.

Ever yours with the feeling of time passing,

Paul Cézanne

In 1886, the artist Paul Cézanne received a novel from his close friend, the writer Émile Zola. The novel, *L'Œuvre* (*His Masterpiece*) follows the life of tortured young painter, Claude Lantier, a character that Cézanne immediately recognized as being based on himself. The artist promptly returned the book with a polite letter of thank you and the two men never spoke again. You can read the letter above.

Friendships are fragile and if we aren't careful, cracks can easily appear. At times, friendships will require maintenance and we must be prepared to put in the hard work that is necessary to preserve them. But in some cases, as we have seen, they cannot be salvaged.

There are many factors which can lead to a friendship breaking. Sometimes it is our own actions which can ruin our relationships with those we hold dear, but sometimes we change, or our friends change and that means a friendship has run its natural course. But we don't always have to part with such finality as Zola and Cézanne, of course!

In letter four of *Address Unknown* we have witnessed a change in Martin which can be attributed to the influence of the ideology he is exposed to in Nazi Germany. In this section we will look further at the impact of propaganda on our individual identities and how this inevitably affects our relationships with others.

ACTIVITY: Propaganda posters

■ **ATL**

- Communication skills: Make inferences and draw conclusions

Propaganda: information that is intended to persuade an audience to accept a particular idea or cause, often by using biased material or by stirring up emotion.

In pairs discuss the following:

1 Is propaganda used in today's world?
2 How does propaganda influence people's ideas and behaviours today? Consider examples from where you live and where you are from.
3 During the Holocaust, how do you think propaganda was used to limit what people knew about what was taking place, both in the country and abroad? Use the internet to find out.

The Nazis used propaganda, in a number of forms, as a tool for shaping the beliefs and attitudes of the German public.

Look at the images below. They are Nazi propaganda posters from the 1930s and 40s. Complete the tasks.

Consider the impact these images may have had on a contemporary audience.

Choose one of the posters to **analyse** and write a paragraph linking it to an aspect of the novella. Make reference to the visual and written texts in your response.

◆ Assessment opportunities

◆ In this activity you have practised skills that are assessed using Criterion A: Analysing, Criterion B: Organizing and Criterion D: Using language.

How are Jews presented in these posters? What does this reveal about Nazi attitudes towards the community? How do these images make you feel?

What is suggested in this poster about the concept of family? What can we infer about the role of women in Nazi Germany? How can we relate this to the novella?

What notions of masculinity are explored here?

Comment on the layout of this poster. How is Hitler presented? What message does this poster convey about power?

5 Friends forever?

ACTIVITY: Letters five to eight

■ ATL

- Communication skills: Read critically and for comprehension; Make effective summary notes for studying
- Collaboration skills: Listen actively to other perspectives and ideas

Work in pairs. Person A will look at the letters sent by Max and Person B will look at those written by Martin.

Annotate in detail the texts you have been allocated. Consider the following:

1 **Summarize** the content of your letters. What do you learn about the state of things in Germany?
2 **Identify** attitudes and ideas that are expressed about the Jewish community in the letters. Highlight and annotate key quotations.
3 **Evaluate** the tone of the letters. Do you notice anything about the dates?
4 **Identify** and **analyse** key quotations linked to the theme of friendship.
5 Can you find any links to what you have learned about propaganda in this chapter? Has your character been **indoctrinated**?
6 What can you interpret about information, censorship and surveillance from the men's communication?

In pairs, share your annotations and analysis and discuss what this reveals about the men's friendship. Together, write two paragraphs comparing the characters of Max and Martin.

◆ Assessment opportunities

- In this activity you have practised skills that are assessed using Criterion A: Analysing; Criterion B: Organizing and Criterion D: Using language.

▼ Links to: Art – Music

Visit the link below and listen to *Carmina Burana* by Carl Orff.

www.youtube.com/watch?v=GXFSK0ogeg4

- Do you recognize the composition? Where have you heard it used?
- How would you describe the tone of the piece?
- What feelings does the music evoke? Explain why.

Carmina Burana premiered in Frankfurt on 8 June 1937. It was initially criticized by the Nazis for having undesirable jazz-like rhythms – a genre of music which was labelled 'degenerate' (immoral or harmful) according to the Nazis. There was even a degenerate music exhibition (*Entartete Musik*) held in 1938 to educate the German public about what types of music were acceptable under the regime and to highlight the dangers the 'wrong' kind of music posed to society.

Throughout history, music has been used to inspire, influence and move people. The Nazis were not oblivious to the power of music and when Orff's composition gained popularity, they realized that there was an opportunity to exploit it for the purpose of propaganda.

EXTENSION

Leni Riefenstahl

Leni Riefenstahl was a German dancer, actress and film director best known for her propaganda films *Triumph of the Will* and *Olympia*, which captured the 1936 Summer Olympics which were held in Berlin. Music plays a prominent role in both films.

Watch Riefenstahl's interview below, in which you can also see excerpts from her films. As you watch, listen to what she has to say about her films being described as propaganda, and consider what her body language suggests about how she is feeling.

www.cbc.ca/player/play/1402988922

ACTIVITY: Jewish stereotypes in literature

ATL

- Communication skills: Read critically and for comprehension

Anti-Semitism is the hostility and prejudice towards people of Jewish faith. Throughout history the community has been vilified in art and literature.

Read the following extracts from two nineteenth-century novels and consider the negative presentation of Jewish characters. Annotate the texts and analyse the language and imagery used by the writers.

In pairs discuss what these descriptions reveal about contemporary attitudes towards Jews. Do these descriptions help perpetuate negative stereotypes of Jews? Why is this problematic?

■ Fagin

'As he glided stealthily along, creeping beneath the shelter of the walls and doorways, the hideous old man seemed like some loathsome reptile, engendered in the slime and darkness through which he moved: crawling forth, by night, in search of some rich offal for a meal.'

Oliver Twist, *by Charles Dickens*

'But it was nothing against him in her judgement that he was a greasy, fawning, pawing, creeping, black-browed rascal, who could not look her full in the face, and whose every word sounded like a lie. There was a twang in his voice which ought to have told her that he was utterly untrustworthy. There was an oily pretence at earnestness in his manner which ought to have told that he was not fit to associate with gentlemen. There was a foulness of demeanour about him which ought to have given to her, as a woman at any rate brought up among ladies, an abhorrence of his society.'

The Eustace Diamonds, *by Anthony Trollope*

◆ Assessment opportunities

- ◆ In this activity you have practised skills that are assessed using Criterion A: Analysing.

ACTIVITY: Letters nine to twelve: Griselle

■ ATL

- Communication skills: Read critically and for comprehension
- Creative-thinking skills: Create original works and ideas

In pairs, create a mind map of what we already know about Griselle.

Read letters nine to twelve and complete the tasks:

1. What do you notice about the name of the art gallery in Max's letters? Why is this significant?
2. Think back to your discussion about the title of the book. With that in mind, **interpret** what the expression means based on Max's words in the following extract:

> '... it has been returned to me, the envelope unopened, marked only addressee unknown, (Adressat Unbekannt). What a darkness those words carry! How can she be unknown? It is surely a message that she has come to harm. They know what has happened to her, those stamped letters say, but I am not to know. She has gone into some sort of void and it will be useless to seek her. All this they tell me in two words, Adressat Unbekannt.'

3. What do you notice about the number of letters sent by each correspondent? What does this and the language used in the letters reveal about the men's state of mind?
4. What aspects of Martin's final letter suggest he has been completely indoctrinated?
5. Look through these letters and use mind maps to collate quotations about Griselle. What kind of person is she? How does she challenge contemporary ideals about women? What IB learner profile attributes does she possess? What feelings about Griselle does the writer evoke and how?
6. What does Martin's letter confirm about what Max suspects about the true meaning of the words 'address unknown'?
7. Imagine you are in Griselle's position; a Jewish woman alone in Munich during the rise of the Nazi Party. Write a letter to Max, describing your experiences.

◆ Assessment opportunities

◆ In this activity you have practised skills that are assessed using Criterion A: Analysing, Criterion B: Organizing, Criterion C: Producing text and Criterion D: Using language.

ACTIVITY: Letters thirteen to nineteen: Betrayal and revenge

■ ATL

- Communication skills: Make inferences and draw conclusions; Read critically and for comprehension
- Critical-thinking skills: Evaluate evidence or argument

Read the final letters between Max and Martin and discuss how Max takes revenge on Martin for failing to help his sister.

Max sends a cablegram knowing that it will be read by others. He does this to arouse suspicion and so that Martin's letters will be monitored by the German authorities. **Interpret** the content of Max's cablegram and letters and explain what impression he wishes to convey to the Nazis. Why does he want to do this? What is the outcome? Make some inferences about why Max's final letter is returned and stamped with the words 'Address Unknown'?

ACTIVITY: Is social media and our increasing use of mobile technology damaging friendships?

■ ATL

- Critical-thinking skills: Evaluate evidence or argument; Gather and organize relevant information to formulate an argument

In Taylor's *Address Unknown*, external pressures culminating in an act of betrayal lead to the breakdown of Max and Martin's friendship. What aspects of life in today's world could affect your friendships?

Some say that we should be wary of technology and social media. Yes, thanks to technical innovation we're more connected than ever before and the world seems like a smaller place. But can it have a contrary effect? Can social media change our friendships for the worse?

Have a debate: *Is social media and our increasing use of mobile technology damaging friendships?*

Split into two teams and gather evidence to formulate your argument. Remember to choose your sources wisely.

◆ Assessment opportunities

- In this activity you have practised skills that are assessed using Criterion D: Using language.

In her novella, Taylor uses the protagonists' communication to demonstrate the power of the written word. Max not only takes revenge against Martin for his betrayal, but also takes a stand against Nazi power. **Evaluate** whether Max's act of revenge is justified.

◆ Assessment opportunities

- In this activity you have practised skills that are assessed using Criterion A: Analysing and Criterion D: Using language.

ACTIVITY: How can we use literature and art to critique social injustice?

■ ATL

- Collaboration skills: Listen actively to other perspectives and ideas

In pairs, reflect on your reading of the novella.

- **Identify** Taylor's purpose for writing the novella.
- **Discuss** the message it conveys about friendship.
- **Evaluate** the structure and genre of the novella. What is the effect of the epistolary narrative?

◆ Assessment opportunities

- In this activity you have practised skills that are assessed using Criterion A: Analysing and Criterion D: Using language.

ACTIVITY: What learner profile attributes should a good friend possess?

■ ATL

- Creative-thinking skills: Create original works and ideas

In pairs, discuss which IB learner profile attributes a good friend should possess.

Now, on your own, **create** a mind map about … your best friend! This should include the IB learner profile attributes they possess (or lack!), their personality, likes, dislikes and physical appearance.

Use your mind map to **create** a character portrait of your best friend. You should aim to write 500–700 words and use language and literary devices to enrich your writing.

◆ Assessment opportunities

- In this activity you have practised skills that are assessed using Criterion B: Organizing and Criterion C: Producing text.

! **Take action: Opportunity to apply learning through action …**

! **Celebrate International Day of Friendship:** The United Nations International Day of Friendship was proclaimed in 2011 by the UN General Assembly with the idea that friendship between peoples, countries, cultures and individuals can inspire peace efforts and build bridges between communities. Find out more by visiting: www.un.org/en/events/friendshipday/index.shtml. Did you know that Winnie the Pooh was named the world's Ambassador of Friendship at the UN by Nane Annan, wife of Secretary-General Kofi Annan? For ideas on how to celebrate, visit: www.liveabout.com/ways-to-celebrate-friendship-day-1385083.

! **Take a stand against prejudice:** Ignorance is usually the main cause behind prejudice so educate, raise awareness and campaign. Search the internet for ideas.

! **Read more Second World War literature:** There's a wealth of literature devoted to this devastating period in our collective history. John Boyne's *The Boy in the Striped Pyjamas* is another great book which takes friendship as its central theme. *The Book Thief* by Markus Zuzak or *Alone in Berlin* by Hans Fallada are also brilliant depictions of civilian life in Nazi Germany.

SOME SUMMATIVE PROBLEMS TO TRY

Use these problems to apply and extend your learning in this chapter. These tasks are designed so that you can evaluate your learning using the Language and Literature criteria.

Task 1: Speech

Write a speech for your peers about the importance of friendship. Somewhere in your speech you must include a famous quotation about friendship. You can find this by doing a search online for **friendship quotations**.

Your speech should be between 500 and 700 words. You have 60 minutes to complete this task.

Task 2: Essay

What lessons can we learn about the nature of friendship from Address Unknown?

Write an essay in response to the question.

Make reference to the text in your essay and organize your writing using PEA paragraphs.

Frame your analysis with an introduction and a conclusion.

You have 60 minutes to complete this task.

EXTENSION

Bookish besties!

Visit the link below and read about the friendships some of the world's best writers had with other writers.

www.huffingtonpost.com/2014/07/07/author-friendships_n_5545074.html

Reflection

In this chapter we have carried out a close study of Kathrine Kressmann Taylor's novella *Address Unknown* and have seen how the **structure** of an epistolary novel can use **communication** to explore different **points of view** and as a tool to critique social injustice in certain contexts. Through the changing **relationships** between the characters in the text, we can explore the themes of friendship and betrayal.

Use this table to reflect on your own learning in this chapter.						
Questions we asked	Answers we found	Any further questions now?				
Factual: What is a friendship? What is a novella? What is an epistolary novel or novella?						
Conceptual: Why does friendship matter? What IB learner profile attributes should a good friend possess? What factors can cause a friendship to break down? Can propaganda really change the way we think about the world?						
Debatable: Is social media and our increasing use of mobile technology damaging friendships?						
Approaches to learning you used in this chapter:	Description – what new skills did you learn?	How well did you master the skills?				
		Novice	Learner	Practitioner	Expert	
Communication skills						
Collaboration skills						
Research skills						
Thinking skills						
Organization skills						
Learner profile attribute(s)	Reflect on the importance of open-mindedness for our learning in this chapter.					
Open-minded						

5 Friends forever?

Creativity | Theme; Point of View | Personal and cultural expression

6 Do girls run the world?

Throughout history women have used **creativity** as a means of **personal and cultural expression**. By looking closely at the **themes** explored in women's literature throughout the ages, we can develop an understanding of history from a female **point of view**.

CONSIDER AND ANSWER THESE QUESTIONS:

Factual: Who was the first female writer to be published?

Conceptual: Why does women's writing matter? What can we learn about women's history through reading women's literature? What can we learn from women's poetry?

Debatable: Do men and women write differently? Why should we read more women's fiction? Why are certain literary genres dominated by male writers?

Now **share and compare** your thoughts and ideas with your partner, or with the whole class.

IN THIS CHAPTER, WE WILL …

- **Find out** who some of the most important women writers are.
- **Explore** what we can learn from women's writing and how it can give us a different point of view on history.
- **Take action** to help end gender inequality and celebrate women's contribution to society.

■ These Approaches to Learning (ATL) skills will be useful …

- Thinking skills
- Collaborative skills
- Organization skills
- Research skills
- Communication skills

● We will reflect on this learner profile attribute …

- Thinker – We use critical and creative-thinking skills to analyse and take responsible action on complex problems.

◆ Assessment opportunities in this chapter:

- Criterion A: Analysing
- Criterion B: Organizing
- Criterion C: Producing text
- Criterion D: Using language

KEY WORDS

| feminism | *nom-de-plume* |

ACTIVITY: How inequality starts before birth

■ ATL

- Collaboration skills: Practise empathy
- Critical-thinking skills: Draw reasonable conclusions and generalizations

Visit the link below and watch the animation.

www.theguardian.com/global-development/video/2016/oct/11/a-girls-life-how-inequality-starts-before-birth-video-international-day-of-the-girl

In pairs, discuss the following:

1 What is the purpose of the video? Who is the target audience? What message is being conveyed?
2 How did it make you feel? Reflect on what you have learned.
3 Which fact or statistic surprised you most? **Explain** why.
4 **Evaluate** how effective the video is at conveying the intended message. **Identify** examples from the video used by the creators to support your answer.
5 **Discuss** what you think could be done to tackle the problem of gender inequality.

◆ Assessment opportunities

- In this activity you have practised skills that are assessed using Criterion A: Analysing.

ⓘ Did you know …

… many women writers in the nineteenth century adopted **noms-de-plume** or **pseudonyms**, which are fictitious names used by authors? Sometimes known as 'pen names', these can conceal a writer's identity. The Brontë sisters, Charlotte, Emily and Anne, published their first books under the pen names of Currer, Ellis and Acton Bell. Mary Ann Evans wrote under the name George Eliot, but was obliged to reveal her identity following the success of her novel *Adam Bede,* which prompted several men to come forward and claim authorship of the book!

The French writer Aurore Dupin published several works under the pseudonym George Sand; Dupin was even known to disguise herself as a man so she could wander freely through the streets of Paris and observe life in the city.

In pairs, discuss the reasons why women might have used pen names. Use the internet to find out more.

If you were to write a novel, what would be your pen name?

6 Do girls run the world?

Why does women's writing matter?

Women make up almost 50 per cent of the world's population, and over the centuries have made a tremendous contribution to all aspects of life, including art. But sadly, women haven't always received the recognition they deserve for their achievements. Women have overcome the obstacles which have lain in their paths and changed the course of history by demanding equality, a voice and a rightful place in their societies, and continue to do so in many parts of the world today.

Hypophora

Most of us are familiar with rhetorical questions (these are questions which don't require an answer, but rather are designed to create a dramatic effect or to encourage the audience to think), but what do you call a question that is immediately answered by the writer themselves?

Questions raised and then immediately answered by the writer are referred to as 'hypophora'. Take, for example, Beyoncé's *'Who run the world? Girls!'* lyric.

This chapter celebrates the contribution women have made in literature and is an inquiry into what women's writing, past and present, and from across the world, can teach us.

ACTIVITY: Words and women

■ ATL

Communication skills: Negotiate ideas and knowledge with peers and teachers

To start, in pairs discuss what you think 'feminism' is. Come up with a definition as a group and then use the internet to help you refine it. Are you a feminist? Should we all be feminists? Discuss.

- Interpret what each of the following quotations means.
- Analyse the thoughts, feelings, ideas or attitudes about women that are being expressed in these quotations.
- Which one do you like the most? Explain why.

'No country can ever truly flourish if it stifles the potential of its women and deprives itself of the contributions of half of its citizens.'

Michelle Obama

'Who run the world? Girls!'

Beyoncé Knowles

'A woman is like a tea bag – you never know how strong she is until she gets into hot water.'

Eleanor Roosevelt

'I myself have never been able to find out precisely what a feminist is. I only know that people call me a feminist whenever I express sentiments that differentiate me from a doormat.'

Rebecca West

'... if we revert to history, we shall find that the women who have distinguished themselves have neither been the most beautiful nor the most gentle of their sex.'

Mary Wollstonecraft

◆ Assessment opportunities

- In this activity you have practised skills that are assessed using Criterion A: Analysing.

What can we learn about women's history through reading women's literature?

WHO WAS THE FIRST FEMALE WRITER TO BE PUBLISHED?

In a country house in the 1930s, something quite remarkable fell out of a cupboard during a search for a ping-pong ball: the only known manuscript of *The Book of Margery Kempe*, a fifteenth-century account of one woman's life. Believed to be one of the earliest examples of published women's writing, the book not only gives us a remarkable insight into life in medieval England, but also shows us that women like Margery were challenging social convention even then by deviating from prescribed 'feminine' roles and duties.

Throughout history, women's lives have been fraught with difficulty, and although we have made great strides towards achieving equality, we still have a long way to go even today. Up until very recently, the achievements and contributions of women have often been overlooked by historians, and reading women's literature is one way in which we can fill in the gaps and develop a deeper understanding of the lives and struggles of women over time.

Despite the odds (literacy, poverty and rigid social norms to name a few), women have always written, and for a number of reasons too. Literature, whether that be poetry, fiction or drama, is a means of personal expression and writing gave women a voice in times where they were often denied one. But for some, writing served a more material purpose; it allowed women a chance to be economically independent. Take for instance seventeenth-century writer Aphra Behn, who wrote to earn money to save herself from debtor's prison. Behn is widely believed to be the first professional writer in English history and, according to Virginia Woolf, 'all women together ought to let flowers fall upon [her tomb], for it was she who earned them the right to speak their minds.'

■ Aphra Behn is often credited with being the first woman writer to earn a living by her pen. She began to make a living by writing plays for the Duke's Theatre, London, but is also known for her novels and poems.

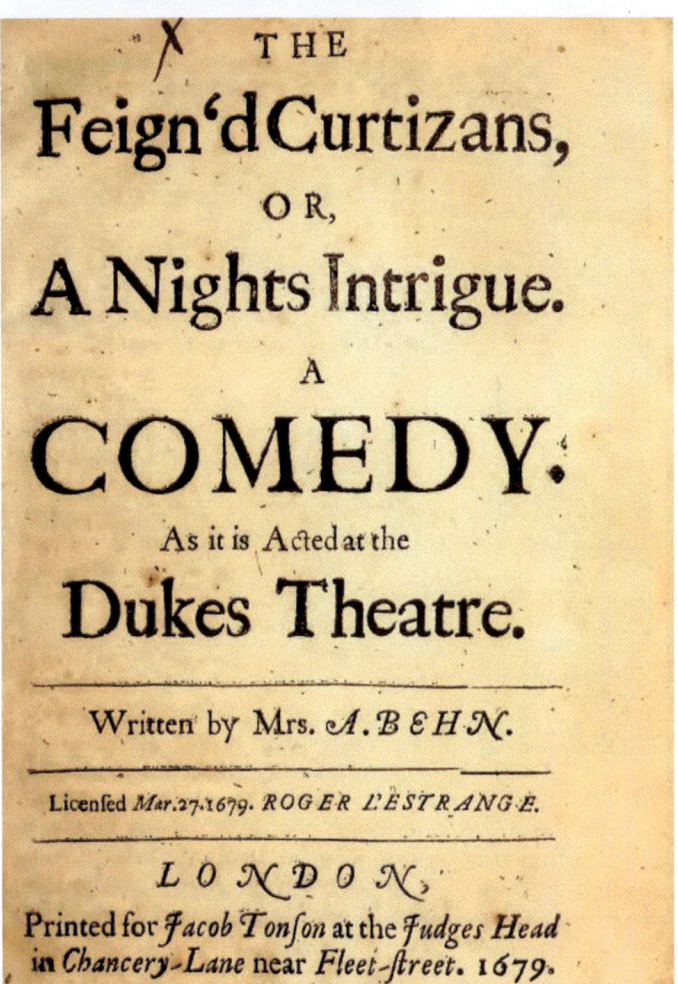

ACTIVITY: What can we learn from reading the work of Jane Austen?

■ ATL

- Communication skills: Take effective notes in class; Read critically and for comprehension

■ 'Give a girl an education and introduce her properly into the world, and ten to one but she has the means of settling well, without further expense to anybody.' Jane Austen

The year 2017 marked the 200th anniversary of Jane Austen's death. Austen is widely considered to be one of the greatest English novelists. Although Austen's novels failed to make her rich, she did make some profit from her writing.

Visit the link below and watch the video. Complete the following tasks:

1. Take notes about what we as readers can learn from Austen's novels. List some of the titles of her novels mentioned in the video.
2. **Summarize** what you learn about Jane Austen's life in a one-paragraph biography.
3. In pairs, **discuss** whether you think any of the issues or lessons referred to in the video are still relevant today.

www.youtube.com/watch?v=LIYiThAyY8s&index=18&list=PLwxNMb28XmpdJpJzF2YRBnfmOva0HE0ZI

Now, read the opening chapter of one of Austen's most popular novels, *Pride and Prejudice*, and complete the tasks that follow.

◆ Assessment opportunities

♦ In this activity you have practised skills that are assessed using Criterion A: Analysing.

> What can you infer from the extract about the position of women in society at the time?

Chapter 1

It is a truth universally acknowledged, that a single man in possession of a good fortune, must be in want of a wife.

However little known the feelings or views of such a man may be on his first entering a neighbourhood, this truth is so well fixed in the minds of the surrounding families, that he is considered the rightful property of some one or other of their daughters.

'My dear Mr. Bennet,' said his lady to him one day, 'have you heard that Netherfield Park is let at last?'

Mr. Bennet replied that he had not.

'But it is,' returned she; 'for Mrs. Long has just been here, and she told me all about it.'

Mr. Bennet made no answer.

'Do you not want to know who has taken it?' cried his wife impatiently.

'You want to tell me, and I have no objection to hearing it.'

This was invitation enough.

'Why, my dear, you must know, Mrs. Long says that Netherfield is taken by a young man of large fortune from the north of England; that he came down on Monday in a chaise and four to see the place, and was so much delighted with it, that he agreed with Mr. Morris immediately; that he is to take possession before Michaelmas, and some of his servants are to be in the house by the end of next week.'

'What is his name?'

'Bingley.'

'Is he married or single?'

'Oh! Single, my dear, to be sure! A single man of large fortune; four or five thousand a year. What a fine thing for our girls!'

'How so? How can it affect them?'

'My dear Mr. Bennet,' replied his wife, 'how can you be so tiresome! You must know that I am thinking of his marrying one of them.'

'Is that his design in settling here?'

'Design! Nonsense, how can you talk so! But it is very likely that he may fall in love with one of them, and therefore you must visit him as soon as he comes.'

> What factors might have influenced a woman's decision to accept or reject a marriage proposal?

> In pairs, discuss why you think women were expected to marry during Austen's time and what the consequences of remaining single might have been. Use the internet to see if you can find out.

> What does the dialogue reveal to us about the characters?

'I see no occasion for that. You and the girls may go, or you may send them by themselves, which perhaps will be still better, for as you are as handsome as any of them, Mr. Bingley may like you the best of the party.'

'My dear, you flatter me. I certainly have had my share of beauty, but I do not pretend to be anything extraordinary now. When a woman has five grown-up daughters, she ought to give over thinking of her own beauty.'

'In such cases, a woman has not often much beauty to think of.'

'But, my dear, you must indeed go and see Mr. Bingley when he comes into the neighbourhood.'

'It is more than I engage for, I assure you.'

'But consider your daughters. Only think what an establishment it would be for one of them. Sir William and Lady Lucas are determined to go, merely on that account, for in general, you know, they visit no newcomers. Indeed you must go, for it will be impossible for us to visit him if you do not.'

'You are over-scrupulous, surely. I dare say Mr. Bingley will be very glad to see you; and I will send a few lines by you to assure him of my hearty consent to his marrying whichever he chooses of the girls; though I must throw in a good word for my little Lizzy.'

'I desire you will do no such thing. Lizzy is not a bit better than the others; and I am sure she is not half so handsome as Jane, nor half so good-humoured as Lydia. But you are always giving her the preference.'

'They have none of them much to recommend them,' replied he; 'they are all silly and ignorant like other girls; but Lizzy has something more of quickness than her sisters.'

'Mr. Bennet, how can you abuse your own children in such a way? You take delight in vexing me. You have no compassion for my poor nerves.'

> What ideas about women are being presented here?

'You mistake me, my dear. I have a high respect for your nerves. They are my old friends. I have heard you mention them with consideration these last twenty years at least.'

'Ah, you do not know what I suffer.'

'But I hope you will get over it, and live to see many young men of four thousand a year come into the neighbourhood.'

'It will be no use to us, if twenty such should come, since you will not visit them.'

'Depend upon it, my dear, that when there are twenty, I will visit them all.'

Mr. Bennet was so odd a mixture of quick parts, sarcastic humour, reserve, and caprice, that the experience of three-and-twenty years had been insufficient to make his wife understand his character. Her mind was less difficult to develop. She was a woman of mean understanding, little information, and uncertain temper. When she was discontented, she fancied herself nervous. The business of her life was to get her daughters married; its solace was visiting and news.

> **Identify** whose voice this is. Comment on the effect of this.

ACTIVITY: *A Room of One's Own*

ATL

- Communication skills: Read critically and for comprehension

The modernist writer Virginia Woolf was an important voice in British literature during the early-twentieth century. Virginia Woolf was an advocate for women's rights and wanted to raise the status of women in society.

In *A Room of One's Own,* her famous 1929 essay on women and fiction, Woolf builds on the premise that 'a woman must have money and a room of her own if she is to write fiction' – '500 a year to be exact', she later clarifies. In pairs, **discuss** and **interpret** what she means.

For Woolf, women were not free to participate fully in life or able to thrive creatively because they were economically oppressed and poorer than their male counterparts. Women didn't have the private space necessary for creative production or the money to support themselves so they could devote their minds and energy to their writing.

In the essay, Woolf takes a chronological journey through centuries of women's literature and in the extract over the page she shares her thoughts on nineteenth-century literature, and the era of the professional woman writer.

Read the extract and complete the tasks.

1. What connections between the female writers of the nineteenth century does Woolf explore in this section?
2. What does Woolf suggest is the reason behind this?
3. Which technique does she use to explore this idea?
4. Can you link this back to her idea that 'a woman must have money and a room of her own if she is to write fiction'?
5. What does Woolf imply about how certain female writers might have developed had their circumstances been different? What is your opinion of this?

◆ Assessment opportunities

- In this activity you have practised skills that are assessed using Criterion A: Analysing.

6 Do girls run the world?   125

Here, then, one had reached the early nineteenth century. And here, for the first time, I found several shelves given up entirely to the works of women. But why, I could not help asking, as I ran my eyes over them, were they, with very few exceptions, all novels? The original impulse was to poetry. The 'supreme head of song' was a poetess. Both in France and in England the women poets precede the women novelists. Moreover, I thought, looking at the four famous names, what had George Eliot in common with Emily Brontë? Did not Charlotte Brontë fail entirely to understand Jane Austen? Save for the possibly relevant fact that not one of them had a child, four more incongruous characters could not have met together in a room – so much so that it is tempting to invent a meeting and a dialogue between them. Yet by some strange force they were all compelled when they wrote, to write novels. Had it something to do with being born of the middle class, I asked; and with the fact, which Miss Emily Davies a little later was so strikingly to demonstrate, that the middle-class family in the early nineteenth century was possessed only of a single sitting-room between them? If a woman wrote, she would have to write in the common sitting-room. And, as Miss Nightingale was so vehemently to complain, – 'women never have an half hour … that they can call their own' – she was always interrupted. Still it would be easier to write prose and fiction there than to write poetry or a play. Less concentration is required. Jane Austen wrote like that to the end of her days. 'How she was able to effect all this', her nephew writes in his Memoir, 'is surprising, for she had no separate study to repair to, and most of the work must have been done in the general sitting-room, subject to all kinds of casual interruptions. She was careful that her occupation should not be suspected by servants or visitors or any persons beyond her own family party. Jane Austen hid her manuscripts or covered them with a piece of blotting-paper. Then, again, all the literary training that a woman had in the early nineteenth century was training in the observation of character, in the analysis of emotion. Her sensibility had been educated for centuries by the influences of the common sitting-room. People's feelings were impressed on her; personal relations were always before her eyes. Therefore, when the middle-class woman took to writing, she naturally wrote novels, even though, as seems evident enough, two of the four famous women here named were not by nature novelists. Emily Brontë should have written poetic plays; the overflow of George Eliot's capacious mind should have spread itself when the creative impulse was spent upon history or biography. They wrote novels, however; one may even go further, I said, taking *Pride and Prejudice* from the shelf, and say that they wrote good novels.

EXTENSION

Project Gutenberg is an online resource which provides access to free electronic books, or eBooks. The project was set up to encourage the creation and distribution of eBooks.

Follow the link below to access more of Virginia Woolf's work. We recommend starting with some of her shorter essays.

http://gutenberg.net.au/pages/woolf.html

ACTIVITY: Women writers – research and presentations

■ ATL

- Information literacy skills: Access information to be informed and inform others
- Communication skills: Read critically and for comprehension

For this task you will carry out extensive research and prepare a detailed presentation for your peers. You can choose from one of the three following options:

1. **Focus on a particular woman writer of your choice.**
2. **Choose a particular time period (century or decade) or movement (for example, Romanticism or the Renaissance) and explore a variety of women writers and texts.**
3. **Explore women writers and writing from a particular country.**

You should spend at least a lesson to carry out extensive research and use a variety of sources. You might want to find out the following (focus on the bullet points most relevant to the option you have selected):

- Biographical information about your selected writer or writers.
- The legacy / history of women's writing and how it may have changed over time.
- Social attitudes at the time towards women and writing.
- Historical context – what was happening at the time that some of these women were writing and their possible influence.
- The genre / genres of writing.
- Key literary works.
- Themes explored in women's writing.
- Publication and reception of the texts.

Your presentation can take any form you please. Evaluate the most suitable way to present the content you have gathered.

In addition to your presentation, you must select a text by your (or one of your) selected writers – this could be a short poem or an extract from a longer text – and analyse and annotate it in detail. Share your text with your peers and guide them through a reading.

◆ Assessment opportunities

◆ In this activity you have practised skills that are assessed using Criterion A: Analysing, Criterion B: Organizing and Criterion D: Using language.

So far in this chapter we have looked at some aspects of the history of women's writing and explored some examples. We have carried out some research about female writers and have considered some of the obstacles they may have faced in times past. Through reading women's writing we have developed an understanding of social and historical contexts and have developed a different point of view on history.

▼ Links to: Visual Arts – women and art

■ (Clockwise from top left) Louise Bourgeois, Tracy Emin, Berthe Morisot, Frida Kahlo and Amrita Sher-Gil are just a few of the many female artists that have made an important contribution to the world of art.

Women have always created art but have often been overshadowed by their male counterparts. Visit the link to the right and read more about how women have to the right represented, underrepresented and misrepresented in art history.

https://www.khanacademy.org/humanities/becoming-modern/introduction-becoming-modern/issues-in-19th-century-art/v/where-are-the-women

Do men and women write differently?

WHY ARE CERTAIN LITERARY GENRES DOMINATED BY MALE WRITERS?

■ Why are female writers under-represented in certain genres?

'Women's writing' is the term often used to describe writing which captures the experiences and history of women. But this is a limiting definition. Women's writing is as diverse as the women who produce and, indeed, consume it. Writing produced by women spans all genres, fiction and non-fiction, but sadly, women writers are still under-represented in some areas.

Over the centuries, women have demonstrated time and time again that they are as capable at writing literature and non-fiction as their male counterparts. Yet some critics believe that there are fundamental differences between the way men and women write. Since the 1970s linguists have developed theories about how men and women use language differently in their social interactions. But there is nothing to suggest that one gender is inherently better equipped to produce high-quality literature.

In this section we will look at the under-representation of women writers in certain genres and explore female presentations of male characters and points of view.

ACTIVITY: Are women writers under-represented in imaginative fiction?

■ ATL

- Communication skills: Read critically and for comprehension
- Collaboration skills: Listen actively to other perspectives and ideas

Read the article in the link below and complete the following tasks:

www.theverge.com/2017/3/8/14835402/science-fiction-without-women-books-mary-shelley-ursula-k-le-guin

1. What did Mary Robinette Kowal find after conducting her informal experiment? Does this surprise you?
2. What point does Liptak make about the target audience for fiction of this genre?
3. What does he suggest about the origins of the genre? Given the subject of our inquiry, why is this significant?
4. What point is made in the article about perspective?
5. Based on the content of the article, discuss how important you think the contribution of female writers is to the genre.
6. What challenges do female writers of imaginative fiction face? Why do you think this is?
7. Have you read any science fiction or fantasy novels? Are they written by men or women? Does this matter? Discuss in groups.

◆ Assessment opportunities

- In this activity you have practised skills that are assessed using Criterion A: Analysing.

ACTIVITY: Read, write, share: Can women write imaginative fiction?

■ ATL

- Communication skills: Read critically and for comprehension; Give and receive meaningful feedback
- Creative-thinking skills: Create original works and ideas
- Organization skills: Set goals that are challenging and realistic

Let's take a look at some examples of imaginative fiction written by women. Read the three extracts starting opposite and complete the tasks.

1. In pairs, **discuss** the genre conventions of imaginative fiction. You can refer to Chapter 3 in *Language & Literature 1* to refresh your memory. How many can you identify in these extracts?
2. For each text **evaluate** how effectively each writer transports you into the world they have created. **Analyse** the language and stylistic choices the writers use to achieve this.
3. **Compare and contrast** the texts. What do they have in common? How do they differ?
4. In pairs, **discuss** which one you enjoyed the most and explain why, making reference to the text.
5. Look again at Ursula Le Guin's *The Dispossessed*. What do you think happens next? Create a mind map of the possibilities then use your ideas to create a narrative description of what happens next. You should aim to write at least one page.
6. Share your writing and evaluate each other's work, and set targets to help you improve next time.

◆ Assessment opportunities

- In this activity you have practised skills that are assessed using Criterion A: Analysing, Criterion B: Organizing, Criterion C: Producing text and Criterion D: Using language.

Dragonworld

by Zhang Xinxin, translated by Helen Wang

As they come to the footbridge, his classmate whips a small hammer out of his trouser pocket, chips a piece of concrete off the pillar and pops it into the dragon's mouth. The dragon chomps with relish, spraying crumbs as it eats. The other dragons rush to snatch the crumbs from the ground, heads down, tails up, dust flying.

Dragons eating concrete? Is this a dream, wonders Zhaishao. He watches in amazement as the dragons gnaw on the pillars. A skirmish breaks out.

The dragons are eating away at the footbridge. As the concrete disappears, all that is left are the steel sinews weaving in and out, up and down, a dense interlocking spiral structure, like a tower of prehistoric fish bones on the beach. A dragon leaps up and bangs its head against it, sending a chunk of concrete crashing down and knocking over a cart full of sand and lime that had been left underneath. The youngsters scramble away as best they can, but the dragons keep their heads down and concentrate on the morsels of concrete. All except Zhaishao's little dragon which grabs hold of his T-shirt, and hauls him out of the sand. He notices a set of coloured bands on its front leg, the same ones he has seen on the girl's wrist! Zhaishao races home and as he runs inside he sees the little silver dragon vanish into the tall block by the footbridge and a dragon shadow appear in the window high up.

The Dispossessed

by Ursula Le Guin

The hatches of the shop closed. The Defense crew turned back, carrying their dead companion; they made no effort to stop the leaders of the crowd who came racing towards the ship, though the foreman, white with shock and rage, cursed them to hell as they ran past, and they swerved to avoid her. Once at the ship, the vanguard of the crowd scattered and stood irresolute. The silence of the ship, the abrupt movements of the huge skeletal gantries, the strange burned look of the ground, the absence of anything in human scale, disoriented them. A blast of steam of gas from something connected with the ship made some of them start; they looked up uneasily at the rockets, vast black tunnels overhead. A siren whooped in warning, far across the field. First one person and then another started back towards the gate. Nobody stopped them. Within ten minutes the field was clear, the crowd scattered out along the road to Abenay. Nothing appeared to have happened, after all.

The passenger watched. He saw the field, and the wall around the field, and far outside the wall the distant slopes of the Ne Theras, speckled with scrub holum and sparse, silvery moonthorn.

All this suddenly rushed dazzling down the screen. The passenger felt his head pressed against the padded rest. It was like a dentist's examination, the head pressed back, the jaw forced open. He could not get his breath, he felt sick, he felt his bowels loosen with fear. His whole body cried out to the enormous forces that had taken hold of him, *Not now, not yet, wait!*

Shikasta

by Doris Lessing

From: NOTES on PLANET SHIKASTA

for GUIDANCE of COLONIAL SERVANTS

Of all of the planets we have colonized totally or in part, this is the richest. Specifically: with the greatest potential for variety and range and profusion of its forms of life. This has always been so, throughout the very many changes it has – the accurate word, we are afraid – suffered. Shikasta tends towards extremes in all things. For instance, it has seen phases of enourmousness: gigantic lifeforms and in a wide variety. It has seen phases of the miniscule. Sometimes these epochs have overlapped. More than once the inhabitants of Shikasta have included creatures so large that one of them could consume the living space of hundreds of their co-inhabitants in a single meal. This example is on the scale of the visible (one might even say the dramatic), for the economy of the planet is such that every lifeform preys on another, is supported by another, and in turn is preyed upon, down to the most minute, the subatomic level. This is not always evident to the creatures themselves, who tend to become obsessed with what they consume, and to forget what in turn consumed them.

Over and over again, a shock or a strain in the peculiarly precarious balance of this planet has called forth an accident, and Shikasta has been virtually denuded of life. Again and again it has been jostling full with genera, and diseased because of it.

This planet is above all one of contrasts and contradictions, because of its in-built stresses. Tension is its essential nature. This is its strength. This is its weakness.

Envoys are requested to remember at all times that they cannot find on Shikasta what they will have become familiar with in other parts of our dominion and which therefore they will have become disposed to expect: very long periods of stasis, epochs of almost unchanging harmonious balance.

For instance. They may care to stand in front of the Model of Shikasta, Scale 3 – scaled, that is to roughly present sizes. (Dominant species half of Canonean size.) This sphere, which you will see as they see it on their mapping and cartographic devices, has the diameter of their average predominant-species size.

ACTIVITY: Can women write believable male characters?

■ ATL

- Communication skills: Read critically and for comprehension
- Critical thinking skills: Evaluate evidence or argument

The writer V.S. Naipaul once said, 'I read a piece of writing and within a paragraph or two I know whether it is by a woman or not.' How far do you agree with this statement? Think about some of the books you have read in the past. How aware were you of the writer's gender when you were reading the text? In pairs, discuss whether you think it is possible to tell whether a text has been written by a man or a woman.

Some critics have suggested that both male and female writers struggle to create characters of the opposite sex, but there are numerous literary texts which completely undermine this theory. Some male writers have written some of the most memorable female characters in history and likewise, many female writers have created authentic, well-developed male characters. Think back to your study of *The Ruby in the Smoke* by Philip Pullman. How successfully does Pullman develop the character of Sally?

Read the short story starting over the page by Nigerian writer Chimamanda Ngozi Adichie and complete the tasks:

1 **Identify** the narrative voice. Whose point of view is the story told from?
2 How does Adichie present the characters of the narrator's parents in her story? **Comment** on her use of language and stylistic choices.
3 **Interpret** what message she is trying to convey about superstition in Nigeria.
4 How does Adichie use time in the story?
5 What do we learn about class?
6 How is the character of the narrator presented in the story? Find some key quotations about his personality and **analyse** them.
7 What connects him to Raphael? What causes the friendship to break?
8 In pairs, **discuss** which IB learner profile attributes the narrator possesses and which he lacks.
9 **Evaluate** how well Adichie, a female writer, creates and develops the character of the narrator, who is male.
10 How far do you agree with V.S. Naipaul's claim that it is possible to tell if a text is written by a woman?

◆ Assessment opportunities

- In this activity you have practised skills that are assessed using Criterion A: Analysing, Criterion B: Organizing and Criterion D: Using language.

6 Do girls run the world?   133

Apollo

by Chimamanda Ngozi Adichie

Twice a month, like a dutiful son, I visited my parents in Enugu, in their small overfurnished flat that grew dark in the afternoon. Retirement had changed them, shrunk them. They were in their late eighties, both small and mahogany-skinned, with a tendency to stoop. They seemed to look more and more alike, as though all the years together had made their features blend and bleed into one another. They even smelled alike – a menthol scent, from the green vial of Vicks VapoRub they passed to each other, carefully rubbing a little in their nostrils and on aching joints. When I arrived, I would find them either sitting out on the veranda overlooking the road or sunk into the living-room sofa, watching Animal Planet. They had a new, simple sense of wonder. They marvelled at the wiliness of wolves, laughed at the cleverness of apes, and asked each other, 'Ifukwa? Did you see that?'

They had, too, a new, baffling patience for incredible stories. Once, my mother told me that a sick neighbor in Abba, our ancestral home town, had vomited a grasshopper – a living, writhing insect, which, she said, was proof that wicked relatives had poisoned him. 'Somebody texted us a picture of the grasshopper,' my father said. They always supported each other's stories. When my father told me that Chief Okeke's young house help had mysteriously died, and the story around town was that the chief had killed the teen-ager and used her liver for moneymaking rituals, my mother added, 'They say he used the heart, too.'

Fifteen years earlier, my parents would have scoffed at these stories. My mother, a professor of political science, would have said 'Nonsense' in her crisp manner, and my father, a professor of education, would merely have snorted, the stories not worth the effort of speech. It puzzled me that they had shed those old selves, and become the kind of Nigerians who told anecdotes about diabetes cured by drinking holy water.

Still, I humored them and half listened to their stories. It was a kind of innocence, this new childhood of old age. They had grown slower with the passing years, and their faces lit up at the sight of me and even their prying questions – 'When will you give us a grandchild? When will you bring a girl to introduce to us?' – no longer made me as tense as before. Each time I drove away, on Sunday afternoons after a big lunch of rice and stew, I wondered if it would be the last time I would see them both alive, if before my next visit I would receive a phone call from one of them telling me to come right away. The thought filled me with a nostalgic sadness that stayed with me until I got back to Port Harcourt. And yet I knew that if I had a family, if I could complain about rising school fees as the children of their friends did, then I would not visit them so regularly. I would have nothing for which to make amends.

During a visit in November, my parents talked about the increase in armed robberies all over the east. Thieves, too, had to prepare for Christmas. My mother told me how a vigilante mob in Onitsha had caught some thieves, beaten them, and torn off their clothes – how old tires had been thrown over their heads like necklaces, amid shouts for petrol and matches, before the police arrived, fired shots in the air to disperse the crowd, and took the robbers away. My mother paused, and I waited for a supernatural detail that would embellish the story. Perhaps, just as they arrived at the police station, the thieves had turned into vultures and flown away.

'Do you know,' she continued, 'one of the armed robbers, in fact the ring leader, was Raphael? He was our houseboy years ago. I don't think you'll remember him.'

I stared at my mother. 'Raphael?'

'It's not surprising he ended like this,' my father said. 'He didn't start well.'

My mind had been submerged in the foggy lull of my parents' storytelling, and I struggled now with the sharp awakening of memory.

My mother said again, 'You probably won't remember him. There were so many of those houseboys. You were young.'

But I remembered. Of course I remembered Raphael.

Nothing changed when Raphael came to live with us, not at first. He seemed like all the others, an ordinary-looking teen from a nearby village. The houseboy before him, Hyginus, had been sent home for insulting my mother. Before Hyginus was John, whom I remembered because he had not been sent away; he had broken a plate while washing it and, fearing my mother's anger, had packed his things and fled before she came home from work. All the houseboys treated me with the contemptuous care of people who disliked my mother. Please come and eat your food, they would say – I don't want trouble from Madam. My mother regularly shouted at them, for being slow, stupid, hard of hearing; even her bell-ringing, her thumb resting on the red knob, the shrillness searing through the house, sounded like shouting. How difficult could it be to remember to fry the eggs differently, my father's plain and hers with onions, or to put the Russian dolls back on the same shelf after dusting, or to iron my school uniform properly?

I was my parents' only child, born late in their lives. 'When I got pregnant, I thought it was menopause,' my mother told me once. I must have been around eight years old, and did not know what 'menopause' meant. She had a brusque manner, as did my father; they had about them the air of people who were quick to dismiss others. They had met at the University of Ibadan, married against their families' wishes – his thought her too educated, while hers preferred a wealthier suitor – and spent their lives in an intense and intimate competition over who published more, who won at badminton, who had the last word in an argument. They often read aloud to each other in the evening, from journals or newspapers, standing rather than sitting in the parlor, sometimes pacing, as though about to spring at a new idea. They drank Mateus rosé – that dark, shapely bottle always seemed to be resting on a table near them – and left behind glasses faint with reddish dregs. Throughout my childhood, I worried about not being quick enough to respond when they spoke to me.

I worried, too, that I did not care for books. Reading did not do to me what it did to my parents, agitating them or turning them into vague beings lost to time, who did not quite notice when I came and went. I read books only enough to satisfy them, and to answer the kinds of unexpected questions that might come in the middle of a meal – What did I think of Pip? Had Ezeulu done the right thing? I sometimes felt like an interloper in our house. My bedroom had bookshelves, stacked with the overflow books that did not fit in the study and the corridor, and they made my stay feel transient, as though I were not quite where I was supposed to be. I sensed my parents' disappointment in the way they glanced at each other when I spoke about a book, and I knew that what I had said was not incorrect but merely ordinary, uncharged with their brand of originality. Going to the staff club with them was an ordeal: I found badminton boring, the shuttlecock seemed to me an unfinished thing, as though whoever had invented the game had stopped halfway.

What I loved was kung fu. I watched 'Enter the Dragon' so often that I knew all the lines, and I longed to wake up and be Bruce Lee. I would kick and strike at the air, at imaginary enemies who had killed my imaginary family. I would pull my mattress onto the floor, stand on two thick books – usually hardcover copies of 'Black Beauty' and 'The Water-Babies' – and leap onto the mattress, screaming 'Haaa!' like Bruce Lee. One day, in the middle of my practice, I looked up to see Raphael standing in the doorway, watching me. I expected a mild reprimand. He had made my bed that morning, and now the room was in disarray. Instead, he smiled, touched his chest, and brought his finger to his tongue, as though tasting his own blood. My favorite scene. I stared at Raphael with the pure thrill of unexpected pleasure. 'I watched the film in the other house where I worked,' he said. 'Look at this.'

He pivoted slightly, leaped up, and kicked, his leg straight and high, his body all taut grace. I was twelve years old and had, until then, never felt that I recognized myself in another person.

Raphael and I practiced in the back yard, leaping from the raised concrete soakaway and landing on the grass. Raphael told me to suck in my belly, to keep my legs straight and my fingers precise. He taught me to breathe. My previous attempts, in the enclosure of my room, had felt stillborn. Now, outside with Raphael, slicing the air with my arms, I could feel my practice become real, with soft grass below and high sky above, and the endless space mine to conquer. This was truly happening. I could become a black belt one day. Outside the kitchen door was a high open veranda, and I wanted to jump off its flight of six steps and try a flying kick. 'No,' Raphael said. 'That veranda is too high.'

On weekends, if my parents went to the staff club without me, Raphael and I watched Bruce Lee videotapes, Raphael saying, 'Watch it! Watch it!' Through his eyes, I saw the films anew; some moves that I had thought merely competent became luminous when he said, 'Watch it!' Raphael knew what really mattered; his wisdom lay easy on his skin. He rewound the sections in which Bruce Lee used a nunchaku, and watched unblinking, gasping at the clean aggression of the metal-and-wood weapon.

'I wish I had a nunchaku,' I said.

'It is very difficult to use,' Raphael said firmly, and I felt almost sorry to have wanted one.

Not long afterward, I came back from school one day and Raphael said, 'See.' From the cupboard he took out a nunchaku – two pieces of wood, cut from an old cleaning mop and sanded down, held together by a spiral of metal springs. He must have been making it for at least a week, in his free time after his housework. He showed me how to use it. His moves seemed clumsy, nothing like Bruce Lee's. I took the nunchaku and tried to swing it, but only ended up with a thump on my chest. Raphael laughed. 'You think you can just start like that?' he said. 'You have to practice for a long time.'

At school, I sat through classes thinking of the wood's smoothness in the palm of my hand. It was after school, with Raphael, that my real life began. My parents did not notice how close Raphael and I had become. All they saw was that I now happened to play outside, and Raphael was, of course, part of the landscape of outside: weeding the garden, washing pots at the water tank. One afternoon, Raphael finished plucking a chicken and interrupted my solo practice on the lawn. 'Fight!' he said. A duel began, his hands bare, mine swinging my new weapon. He pushed me hard. One end hit him on the arm, and he looked surprised and then impressed, as if he had not thought me capable. I swung again and again. He feinted and dodged and kicked. Time collapsed. In the end, we were both panting and laughing. I remember, even now, very clearly, the smallness of his shorts that afternoon, and how the muscles ran wiry like ropes down his legs.

On weekends, I ate lunch with my parents. I always ate quickly, dreaming of escape and hoping that they would not turn to me with one of their test questions. At one lunch, Raphael served white disks of boiled yam on a bed of greens, and then cubed pawpaw and pineapple.

'The vegetable was too tough,' my mother said. 'Are we grass-eating goats?' She glanced at him. 'What is wrong with your eyes?'

It took me a moment to realize that this was not her usual figurative lambasting—'What is that big object blocking your nose?' she would ask, if she noticed a smell in the kitchen that he had not. The whites of Raphael's eyes were red. A painful, unnatural red. He mumbled that an insect had flown into them.

'It looks like Apollo,' my father said.

My mother pushed back her chair and examined Raphael's face. 'Ah-ah! Yes, it is. Go to your room and stay there.'

Raphael hesitated, as though wanting to finish clearing the plates.

'Go!' my father said. 'Before you infect us all with this thing.'

Raphael, looking confused, edged away from the table. My mother called him back. 'Have you had this before?'

'No, Madam.'

'It's an infection of your conjunctiva, the thing that covers your eyes,' she said. In the midst of her Igbo words, 'conjunctiva' sounded sharp and dangerous. 'We're going to buy medicine for you. Use it three times a day and stay in your room. Don't cook until it clears.' Turning to me, she said, 'Okenwa, make sure you don't go near him. Apollo is very infectious.' From her perfunctory tone, it was clear that she did not imagine I would have any reason to go near Raphael.

Later, my parents drove to the pharmacy in town and came back with a bottle of eye drops, which my father took to Raphael's room in the boys' quarters, at the back of the house, with the air of someone going reluctantly into battle. That evening, I went with my parents to Obollo Road to buy akara for dinner; when we returned, it felt strange not to have Raphael open the front door, not to find him closing the living-room curtains and turning on the lights. In the quiet kitchen, our house seemed emptied of life. As soon as my parents were immersed in themselves, I went out to the boys' quarters and knocked on Raphael's door. It was ajar. He was lying on his back, his narrow bed pushed against the wall, and turned when I came in, surprised, making as if to get up. I had never been in his room before. The exposed light bulb dangling from the ceiling cast sombre shadows.

'What is it?' he asked.

'Nothing. I came to see how you are.'

He shrugged and settled back down on the bed. 'I don't know how I got this. Don't come close.'

But I went close.

'I had Apollo in Primary 3,' I said. 'It will go quickly, don't worry. Have you used the eye drops this evening?'

He shrugged and said nothing. The bottle of eye drops sat unopened on the table.

'You haven't used them at all?' I asked.

'No.'

'Why?'

He avoided looking at me. 'I cannot do it.'

Raphael, who could disembowel a turkey and lift a full bag of rice, could not drip liquid medicine into his eyes. At first, I was astonished, then amused, and then moved. I looked around his room and was struck by how bare it was – the bed pushed against the wall, a spindly table, a gray metal box in the corner, which I assumed contained all that he owned.

'I will put the drops in for you,' I said. I took the bottle and twisted off the cap.

'Don't come close,' he said again.

I was already close. I bent over him. He began a frantic blinking.

'Breathe like in kung fu,' I said.

I touched his face, gently pulled down his lower left eyelid, and dropped the liquid into his eye. The other lid I pulled more firmly, because he had shut his eyes tight.

'Ndo,' I said. 'Sorry.'

He opened his eyes and looked at me, and on his face shone something wondrous. I had never felt myself the subject of admiration. It made me think of science class, of a new maize shoot growing greenly toward light. He touched my arm. I turned to go.

'I'll come before I go to school,' I said.

In the morning, I slipped into his room, put in his eye drops, and slipped out and into my father's car, to be dropped off at school.

By the third day, Raphael's room felt familiar to me, welcoming, uncluttered by objects. As I put in the drops, I discovered things about him that I guarded closely: the early darkening of hair above his upper lip, the ringworm patch in the hollow between his jaw and his neck. I sat on the edge of his bed and we talked about 'Snake in the Monkey's Shadow.' We had discussed the film many times, and we said things that we had said before, but in the quiet of his room they felt like secrets. Our voices were low, almost hushed. His body's warmth cast warmth over me.

He got up to demonstrate the snake style, and afterward, both of us laughing, he grasped my hand in his. Then he let go and moved slightly away from me.

'This Apollo has gone,' he said.

His eyes were clear. I wished he had not healed so quickly.

I dreamed of being with Raphael and Bruce Lee in an open field, practicing for a fight. When I woke up, my eyes refused to open. I pried my lids apart. My eyes burned and itched. Each time I blinked, they seemed to produce more pale ugly fluid that coated my lashes. It felt as if heated grains of sand were under my eyelids. I feared that something inside me was thawing that was not supposed to thaw.

My mother shouted at Raphael, 'Why did you bring this thing to my house? Why?' It was as though by catching Apollo he had conspired to infect her son. Raphael did not respond. He never did when she shouted at him. She was standing at the top of the stairs, and Raphael was below her.

'How did he manage to give you Apollo from his room?' my father asked me.

'It wasn't Raphael. I think I got it from somebody in my class,' I told my parents.

'Who?' I should have known my mother would ask. At that moment, my mind erased all my classmates' names.

'Who?' she asked again.

'Chidi Obi,' I said finally, the first name that came to me. He sat in front of me and smelled like old clothes.

'Do you have a headache?' my mother asked.

'Yes.'

My father brought me Panadol. My mother telephoned Dr. Igbokwe. My parents were brisk. They stood by my door, watching me drink a cup of Milo that my father had made. I drank quickly. I hoped that they would not drag an armchair into my room, as they did every time I was sick with malaria, when I would wake up with a bitter tongue to find one parent inches from me, silently reading a book, and I would will myself to get well quickly, to free them.

Dr. Igbokwe arrived and shined a torch in my eyes. His cologne was strong; I could smell it long after he'd gone, a heady scent close to alcohol that I imagined would worsen nausea. After he left, my parents created a patient's altar by my bed – on a table covered with cloth, they put a bottle of orange Lucozade, a blue tin of glucose, and freshly peeled oranges on a plastic tray. They did not bring the armchair, but one of them was home throughout the week that I had Apollo. They took turns putting in my eye drops, my father more clumsily than my mother, leaving sticky liquid running down my face. They did not know how well I could put in the drops myself. Each time they raised the bottle above my face, I remembered the look in Raphael's eyes that first evening in his room, and I felt haunted by happiness.

My parents closed the curtains and kept my room dark. I was sick of lying down. I wanted to see Raphael, but my mother had banned him from my room, as though he could somehow make my condition worse. I wished that he would come and see me. Surely he could pretend to be putting away a bedsheet, or bringing a bucket to the bathroom. Why didn't he come? He had not even said sorry to me. I strained to hear his voice, but the kitchen was too far away and his voice, when he spoke to my mother, was too low.

Once, after going to the toilet, I tried to sneak downstairs to the kitchen, but my father loomed at the bottom of the stairs.

'Kedu?' He asked. 'Are you all right?'

'I want water,' I said.

'I'll bring it. Go and lie down.'

Finally, my parents went out together. I had been sleeping, and woke up to sense the emptiness of the house. I hurried downstairs and to the kitchen. It, too, was empty. I wondered if Raphael was in the boys' quarters; he was not supposed to go to his room during the day, but maybe he had, now that my parents were away. I went out to the open veranda. I heard Raphael's voice before I saw him, standing near the tank, digging his foot into the sand, talking to Josephine, Professor Nwosu's house help. Professor Nwosu sometimes sent eggs from his poultry, and never let my parents pay for them. Had Josephine brought eggs? She was tall and plump; now she had the air of someone who had already said goodbye but was lingering. With her, Raphael was different – the slouch in his back, the agitated foot. He was shy. She was talking to him with a kind of playful power, as though she could see through him to things that amused her. My reason blurred.

'Raphael!' I called out.

He turned. 'Oh. Okenwa. Are you allowed to come downstairs?'

He spoke as though I were a child, as though we had not sat together in his dim room.

'I'm hungry! Where is my food?' It was the first thing that came to me, but in trying to be imperious I sounded shrill.

Josephine's face puckered, as though she were about to break into slow, long laughter. Raphael said something that I could not hear, but it had the sound of betrayal. My parents drove up just then, and suddenly Josephine and Raphael were roused. Josephine hurried out of the compound, and Raphael came toward me. His shirt was stained in the front, orangish, like palm oil from soup. Had my parents not come back, he would have stayed there mumbling by the tank; my presence had changed nothing.

'What do you want to eat?' he asked.

'You didn't come to see me.'

'You know Madam said I should not go near you.'

Why was he making it all so common and ordinary? I, too, had been asked not to go to his room, and yet I had gone, I had put in his eye drops every day.

'After all, you gave me the Apollo,' I said.

'Sorry.' He said it dully, his mind elsewhere.

I could hear my mother's voice. I was angry that they were back. My time with Raphael was shortened, and I felt the sensation of a widening crack.

'Do you want plantain or yam?' Raphael asked, not to placate me but as if nothing serious had happened. My eyes were burning again. He came up the steps. I moved away from him, too quickly, to the edge of the veranda, and my rubber slippers shifted under me. Unbalanced, I fell. I landed on my hands and knees, startled by the force of my own weight, and I felt the tears coming before I could stop them. Stiff with humiliation, I did not move.

My parents appeared.

'Okenwa!' my father shouted.

I stayed on the ground, a stone sunk in my knee. 'Raphael pushed me.'

'What?' My parents said it at the same time, in English. 'What?'

There was time. Before my father turned to Raphael, and before my mother lunged at him as if to slap him, and before she told him to go pack his things and leave immediately, there was time. I could have spoken. I could have cut into that silence. I could have said that it was an accident. I could have taken back my lie and left my parents merely to wonder.

Why should we read women's literature?

CAN LITERATURE GIVE WOMEN A VOICE?

- 'So let us wage a glorious struggle against illiteracy, poverty and terrorism, let us pick up our books and our pens, they are the most powerful weapons.' Malala Yousafzai

- Too close for comfort? Margaret Atwood's terrifying vision of a world stripped of rights for women.

'This isn't a story I'm telling. It's also a story I'm telling, in my head, as I go along. Tell, rather than write, because I have nothing to write with and writing is in any case forbidden. But if it's a story, even in my head, I must be telling it to someone. You don't tell a story only to yourself. There's always someone else.'

The Handmaid's Tale, Margaret Atwood, 1985

In her chilling dystopian novel, *The Handmaid's Tale*, Canadian writer Margaret Atwood presents us with a world in which women are denied the right to read and write. Sadly, Atwood's Gilead, isn't a far cry from some places in our wold today. The Taliban, for instance, during their occupation in Afghanistan and Pakistan imposed restrictions on education, and particularly opposed the education of girls; Malala Yousafzai, a Pakistani activist for female education, is a living reminder of just how far the Taliban were willing to go to prevent girls from learning.

In 2012, Malala was shot in the head by the Taliban in an attempt to silence her. She survived the horrific attack and in a speech to the UN General Assembly stated that: 'The extremists are afraid of books and pens. The power of education frightens them. They are afraid of women. The power of the voice of women frightens them.'

For women around the world literature has been, and is, a means of self-expression. Writing can be a form of protest or an outlet for sadness or rage. It can be triumphant, celebratory and can empower both writers and readers alike.

ACTIVITY: Mirman Baheer

■ ATL

- Critical thinking skills: Draw reasonable conclusions and generalizations

Visit the link to watch the video about Mirman Baheer, the Afghanistan-based Ladies Literary Society. Members of the Society write and recite *landai*, two-line folk poems. Traditionally, poems of this type have dealt with love and grief, but *landai* produced by women today address a variety of themes and issues.

https://www.youtube.com/watch?v=1XMlT9ST4n8

As you watch, note down the answers to the following questions:

1 What do these poems allow women to do?
2 What do you learn about the way the poems are written and collated?
3 Why do they have to keep their poems a secret?
4. What themes or issues do the women write about?
5 What consequences would the women face if they were caught? Why do they take such great risks?

◆ Assessment opportunities

◆ In this activity you have practised skills that are assessed using Criterion A: Analysing.

6 Do girls run the world?

FLIRT – interpreting poetry

Reading a poem on your own can be difficult if you're not quite sure what to look for. Use the following guide to help you.

1 **F is for 'form':** Before you start exploring the deeper meanings, just take a look at the way the poem is laid out on the page. Is it divided into stanzas? If so, how many? Are they the same length? Does the writer use sentences of a particular type or mood? Is each sentence contained in a single line or do they 'run on'? Once you've answered these questions, then you can start to ask why the writer has made these choices.

2 **L is for 'language':** Look closely at the words the writer uses. Can you identify any patterns or semantic fields? **Analyse** the language. What are the connotations of some of the words?

3 **I is for 'imagery':** What images can you identify? Are they literal or symbolic? Are there any recurring images in the poem? **Interpret** what they might mean and consider their effect on the reader.

4 **R is for 'rhythm and rhyme':** Read the poem out loud and see if it has a rhythm or beat. Do the lines rhyme? Is the rhythm and rhyme regular or irregular? What is the effect of this?

5 **T is for 'tone':** How would you describe the tone of the poem? Is it sad? Happy? Angry?

ACTIVITY: Poetry and pain

ATL

- Communication skills: Read critically and for comprehension
- Information literacy skills: Access information to be informed and inform others
- Collaboration skills: Practise empathy

In Chapter 3, we briefly touched upon the cathartic power of poetry. For centuries, writers – male and female – have used verse to articulate their thoughts and feelings. It is inevitable that we will all experience pain at some point during our lives. Reading the work of others not only teaches us to exercise empathy, but can help us come to terms with our own emotional turmoil.

Read the four poems starting on the opposite page and complete the tasks.

1 **Use** the internet to find some information about the authors and the context surrounding the poems. Consider when they were written and what was going on in the women's lives and in the world around them.
2 **Identify** the message each poem is trying to convey.
3 **Compare and contrast** the poems. What connections can you identify? How do they differ? Use the box to the left on this page to help you.
4 What type of pain is being expressed in each poem?
5 Choose one of the poems and write two to three PEA paragraphs on how language and imagery is used to explore the theme of pain.

◆ Assessment opportunities

- In this activity you have practised skills that are assessed using Criterion A: Analysing, Criterion B: Organizing and Criterion D: Using language.

Aaj Aakhan Waris Shah Nu

I say to Waris Shah today, speak from your grave
And add a new page to your book of love
Once one daughter of Punjab wept, and you wrote your long saga;
Today thousands weep, calling to you Waris Shah:

Arise, o friend of the afflicted; arise and see the state of Punjab,
Corpses strewn on fields, and the Chenaab flowing with much blood.

Someone filled the five rivers with poison,
And this same water now irrigates our soil.

Where was lost the flute, where the songs of love sounded?
And all Ranjha's brothers forgotten to play the flute.

Blood has rained on the soil, graves are oozing with blood,
The princesses of love cry their hearts out in the graveyards.

Today all the Quaido'ns have become the thieves of love and beauty,
Where can we find another one like Waris Shah?

Waris Shah! I say to you, speak from your grave
And add a new page to your book of love.

Amrita Pritam

> Who is the poem addressed to and why?

> What semantic field has been built up in the poem? What is the effect of the imagery in the poem?

Do you find out who the narrator of the poem is? How does she feel?

In the Glass Coffin

Today, I withstood agony again,
Because my life is still lingering,
Trapped in scarcely visible sorrow.
If my body is trapped
Like the life of a dinky, dinky thing,
What is with all this sorrow, this pain?
Like the bygone prince,
Who had loved the forbidden woman,
I believed I would live if I danced in the glass coffin;
I heard I would live with joy
Even in this dim sorrow,
If I worked, studied, and loved.
And so I have lived in this untrustworthy world.
Now, what shall I do with this suffocating feeling
That is burgeoning in this scarcely visible sorrow?
Stupid I! Stupid I!

Kim Myeong-sun

Comment on the use of fairytale elements.

How is the writer feeling? What are the connotations of these words?

To a Wreath of Snow

O transient voyager of heaven!
O silent sign of winter skies!
What adverse wind thy sail has driven
To dungeons where a prisoner lies?

Methinks the hands that shut the sun
So sternly from this mourning brow
Might still their rebel task have done
And checked a thing so frail as thou.

They would have done it had they known
The talisman that dwelt in thee,
For all the suns that ever shone
Have never been so kind to me.

For many a week, and many a day,
My heart was weighed with sinking gloom,
When morning rose in mourning grey
And faintly lit my prison room;

But, angel like, when I awoke,
Thy silvery form so soft and fair,
Shining through darkness, sweetly spoke
Of cloudy skies and mountains bare –

The dearest to a mountaineer,
Who, all life long has loved the snow
That crowned her native summits drear.
Better, than greenest plains below.

And, voiceless, soulless messenger,
Thy presence waked a thrilling tone
That comforts me while thou art here
And will sustain when thou art gone.

Emily Jane Brontë

What alleviates the writer's pain? What does this suggest about the power of nature?

What qualities does the snow possess? Identify and analyse the literary device the writer uses in stanza five. What effect does it create?

Identify and analyse the literary device of the poem's title. What does it reveal about the relationship she is writing about in this poem?

Sweet Torture

My melancholy was gold dust in your hands;
On your long hands I scattered my life;
My sweetnesses remained clutched in your hands;
Now I am a vial of perfume, emptied

How much sweet torture quietly suffered,
When, my soul wrested with shadowy sadness,
She who knows the tricks, I passed the days
kissing the two hands that stifled my life

Alfonsina Storni

What is the effect of the imagery in the poem?

! **Take action: Opportunity to apply learning through action …**

! **Celebrate International Women's Day:** Celebrated every year on 8 March, International Women's Day is a global day celebrating the social, economic, cultural and political achievements of women. The organization is also dedicated to putting an end to gender inequality. Encourage your school to organize some events to mark the occasion. Visit the link for some ideas on how you could take part: www.internationalwomensday.com/resources/

! **Read more women's literature:** Use the internet to find more women writers to read. Type in *top women writers* and access their work at a library or on Project Gutenberg.

Oxymoron

■ *The Scream*, Edvard Munch, 1893

An **oxymoron** is a literary device where two opposite or contradictory ideas are placed together to create an effect.

Take for example the following sentence.

> She screamed in silence.

Of course, what is being described here is an impossibility; it is not possible to scream in silence, so clearly the writer is trying to communicate a deeper message about how the subject of the sentence is feeling. As readers, it is our job to interpret the sentence and extract the meaning.

How do you think she is feeling? Why is her scream silent?

To the Young Wife

Are you content, you pretty three-years' wife?
Are you content and satisfied to live
On what your loving husband loves to give,
And give to him your life?

Are you content with work, — to toil alone,
To clean things dirty and to soil things clean;
To be a kitchen-maid, be called a queen, —
Queen of a cook-stove throne?

Are you content to reign in that small space —
A wooden palace and a yard-fenced land —
With other queens abundant on each hand,
Each fastened in her place?

Are you content to rear your children so?
Untaught yourself, untrained, perplexed, distressed,
Are you so sure your way is always best?
That you can always know?

Have you forgotten how you used to long
In days of ardent girlhood, to be great,
To help the groaning world, to serve the state,
To be so wise — so strong?

And are you quite convinced this is the way,
The only way a woman's duty lies —
Knowing all women so have shut their eyes?
Seeing the world to-day?

Having no dream of life in fuller store?
Of growing to be more than that you are?
Doing the things you know do better far,
Yet doing others — more?

Losing no love, but finding as you grew
That as you entered upon nobler life
You so became a richer, sweeter wife,
A wiser mother too?

What holds you? Ah, my dear, it is your throne,
Your paltry queenship in that narrow place,
Your antique labours, your restricted space,
Your working all alone!

Be not deceived! 'Tis not your wifely bond
That holds you, nor the mother's royal power,
But selfish, slavish service hour by hour —
A life with no beyond!

Charlotte Anna Perkins Gilman

A SUMMATIVE PROBLEM TO TRY

Use this task to apply and extend your learning in this chapter. This task is designed so that you can evaluate your learning using the Language and Literature criteria.

Task

Best known for her short story *The Yellow Wallpaper*, Charlotte Perkins Gilman was a prominent activist and author who did much to promote the cause of women's rights in her writing.

Read her poem *To The Young Wife* (1893), and carry out a close reading of the text, focusing on how Gilman uses language and stylistic choices to express a message about women's rights. If you get stuck, you can refer to the Approaches to Learning skills boxes on pages 15 and 144 (FLIRT).

Comment on and include evidence from the text.

You should aim to write three to four PEA paragraphs.

Reflection

In this chapter we have celebrated and explored women's literature, both past and present, and from across the globe. Through studying a range of texts and the **themes** explored in women's writing, we have developed an understanding of the difficulties women have faced over the centuries and those that they continue to struggle against. In addition we have used literature to see history from the **point of view** of women, and have seen how, despite the odds, women have always used **creativity** as a means of **personal and cultural expression**.

Use this table to reflect on your own learning in this chapter.						
Questions we asked	Answers we found	Any further questions now?				
Factual: Who was the first female writer to be published?						
Conceptual: Why does women's writing matter? What can we learn about women's history through reading women's literature? What can we learn from women's poetry?						
Debatable: Do men and women write differently? Why should we read more women's fiction? Why are certain literary genres dominated by male writers?						
Approaches to learning you used in this chapter:	Description – what new skills did you learn?	How well did you master the skills?				
		Novice	Learner	Practitioner	Expert	
Thinking skills						
Collaborative skills						
Organization skills						
Research skills						
Communication skills						
Learner profile attribute(s)	Reflect on the importance of thinking for your learning in this chapter.					
Thinker						

Glossary

abstract noun An idea, quality, or state rather than a concrete object, for example, love, happiness.

alliteration The repetition of sounds in a sentence or a line.

anachronism Something that is mistakenly placed in a time period where it doesn't belong.

analepsis When a narrator flashes back to an event in the past.

annotation Notes or comments which you make about a text (or image) while reading it.

biography A genre of non-fiction; a written account of someone's life.

chapter A main division of a book that typically has a number and/or a title.

colloquial language The use of everyday language and expressions in conversation.

connotation The associations that a word or image has; implied meanings.

context Something that affects the meaning outside of the text, such as its time period, or country.

determiner Words which appear before a noun to determine who owns it.

dialogue A conversation between two or more people; what is said by the characters.

direct address Using personal pronouns to directly involve the audience.

dramatis personae A list of the characters in a play.

epistolary From the word 'epistle', a form of writing directed to a person or group of people.

foreshadowing When a narrator hints at events which are going to take place as the plot unfolds.

genre Different types of texts and films.

haiku A Japanese poem which consists of three lines and seventeen syllables.

harpy In Greek and Roman mythology, a harpy was a monstrous personification of storm winds. A harpy is often depicted as having a woman's head and body and a bird's wings and claws.

hyperbole Extreme exaggeration used to enhance the effect of a statement.

hypophora Question raised and then immediately answered by the writer.

imagery Very descriptive words that build an image, or picture, in the reader's mind.

indoctrination The process of teaching a person or group to accept a set of beliefs uncritically.

irony Use of words to give a meaning that is different from its literal meaning.

jargon Topic-specific words which may only be understood by subject specialists.

juxtaposition Where two ideas are put together to show a contrast.

masque Also known as masquerade; a form of festive courtly entertainment which was popular in sixteenth- and seventeenth-century Europe.

metaphor A literary technique which allows us to say that a person, place, animal or thing is something else, rather than just similar to it.

monosyllabic lexis Short words, usually made up of a single syllable, which appear frequently in a single text.

motif A recurring idea or image in a story.

narrative A story or account of events.

novella A fictional tale in prose, intermediate in length and complexity between a short story and a novel, and usually concentrating on a single event or chain of events, with a surprising turning point.

omniscient A narrator that has knowledge of all times, people, places, and events, including all characters' thoughts.

onomatopoeia Words that sound like their meaning for example crash, POW, bang.

oxymoron Literary device where opposite or contradictory ideas are placed together to create an effect.

personification A literary technique used to give inanimate objects or concepts human characteristics.

perspective The author's point of view within a text.

presentational devices Features which are used in addition to the writing in a text.

polysyllabic lexis Long words made up of two or more syllables, which appear less frequently in a text.

prolepsis When a narrator flashes forward to an event which hasn't occurred yet.

pronoun Words which replace nouns in sentences.

prose Written or spoken language presented in an ordinary way.

pseudonym A fictitious name used by an author for anonymity.

purpose The writer's reason for writing.

quotation When you refer to the exact words, phrases or sentences from a text.

register The way that we change the way we speak or write to suit our purpose or the context we are in.

repetition Words or phrases that are repeated for effect.

rhyme A repetition of similar-sounding words occurring usually at the end of line in a poem or song.

rhythm The beat of a poem.

rule of three A list of three words of the same word class used for emphasis and effect.

semantic field Language linked to a particular topic or subject.

sibilance The repetition of sibilant sounds (s, sh, z) for effect.

simile A way of describing something by comparing it to something else, often using the word 'like' or 'as'.

soliloquy Where a character speaks their thoughts aloud, usually (but not always) when they are alone.

syllable A part of a word that is pronounced with one uninterrupted sound.

symbolism When an item symbolises, or represents, something else, for example a heart symbolises love.

synonym Word that is the same in meaning to another word.

tone The emotion or feelings that a text creates.

verse A type of writing which is arranged in a rhythm and typically has a rhyme.

Acknowledgements

The Publishers would like to thank the following for permission to reproduce copyright material. Every effort has been made to trace all copyright holders, but if any have been inadvertently overlooked the Publishers will be pleased to make the necessary arrangements at the first opportunity.

Photo credits

p.2 © Philip Pullman, 1999, 2004, 2006, 2009, 2012, 2015, 2016, Reproduced with the permission of Scholastic Ltd, All Rights Reserved; **p.3** © Brian Jackson/stock.adobe.com; **p.4** © Cliff Hide Local/Alamy Stock Photo; **p.7** © Guy Harrop/Alamy Stock Photo; **p.9** *l* © BBC/AF archive/Alamy Stock Photo, *r* © Classic Collection/Alamy Stock Photo; **p.11** *l* © V&A Images/Alamy Stock Photo, *r* © Lanmas/Alamy Stock Photo; **p13** *tr* © Wikicommons; **p.14** *l* © Lebrecht Music and Arts Photo Library/Alamy Stock Photos, *r* © World History Archive/Alamy Stock Photo; **p.15** ©WavebreakMediaMicro/stock.adobe.com; **p.18** *t* © Paul Fearn/Alamy Stock Photo, *b* © Johnny Greig/Alamy Stock Photo; **p.19** Retribution, 1858 (oil on canvas), Armitage, Edward (1817-96) / Leeds Museums and Galleries (Leeds Art Gallery) U.K. / Bridgeman Images; **p.21** © Photo12/Ann Ronan Picture Library/Alamy Stock Photo; **p.22** © Chronicle/Alamy Stock Photo; **p.23** © Moviestore collection Ltd/Alamy Stock Photo; **p.24** *t* © Contraband Collection/Alamy Stock Photo, *b* © 19th era/Alamy Stock Photo; **p.25** *t* © Classic Image/Alamy Stock Photo, *b* © The Granger Collection/Alamy Stock Photo; **p.26** *tl* © HIP/Topfoto, *cl* © Elena Chaykina/Alamy Stock Photo, *r* © A group of Lascars (sailors). They are described as Bengali, Malay and Siamese. / British Library, London, UK / © British Library Board. All Rights Reserved / Bridgeman Images; **p.27** *tl* © Chronicle/Alamy Stock Photo, *cl* © Paul Doyle/Alamy Stock Photo; **p.29** *t* © Granger Historical Picture Archive/Alamy Stock Photo, *b* © Lebrecht Music and Arts Photo Library/Alamy Stock Photo; **p.30** *tl* © Oote Boe 2/Alamy Stock Photo, *tr* © Tomas Abad/Alamy Stock Photo, *b* © Archivart/Alamy Stock Photo; **p.32** © Chris Titze Imaging/stock.adobe.com; **p.33** © BillionPhotos.com/stock.adobe.com; **p.34** *l* © ITAR-TASS Photo Agency/Alamy Stock Photo, *r* © Francis Specker/Alamy Stock Photo; **p.36** *tr* © Lebrecht Music and Arts Photo Library/Alamy Stock Photo, *br* © PAINTING/Alamy Stock Photo; **p.37** *t* ©2003 Credit:Topham Picturepoint/Topfoto, *c* © MARKA/Alamy Stock Photo, *b* © Daiju Kitamura AFLO SPORT 1045/Aflo Co., Ltd./Alamy Stock Photo; **p.47** © Cristian Barnett/The National Trust Photolibrary/Alamy Stock Photo; **p.49** © Pictorial Press Ltd/Alamy Stock Photo; **p.51** *t* © Pictorial Press Ltd/Alamy Stock Photo, *b* © Courtesy: CSU Archives/Everett Collection/Alamy Stock Photos; **p.52** © Reuben Singh/The India Today Group/Getty Images; **p.53** *l* © Everett Collection Inc/Alamy Stock Photo, *r* © Cineclassico/Alamy Stock Photo; **p.56** *t* © Yossarian6/stock.adobe.com, © Monkey Business/stock.adobe.com; **p.57** © Lukas Gojda/stock.adobe.com, *b* © Monkey Business/stock.adobe.com; **p.58** © Moviestore collection Ltd/Alamy Stock Photo; **p.59** *bl* The New Zealand Herald, *br* © D. Long/Globe Photos/ZUMA Press, Inc./Alamy Stock Photo, *tr* © One photo/Shutterstock.com; **p.60** *c* © Rafael Ben-Ari/Alamy Stock Photo, *t* © Wenra/Shutterstock.com; **p.62** *l* © Granger Historical Picture Archive/Alamy Stock Photo, *r* © Paul Fearn/Alamy Stock Photo; **p.64** © Classic Image/Alamy Stock Photo; **p.66** © Jeff Vespa/WireImage/Getty Images; **p.68** © Lebrecht Music and Arts Photo Library/Alamy Stock Photo; **p.70** © World History Archive/Alamy Stock Photo; **p.73** *tl* © Dmitriy Syechin/stock.adobe.com, *bl* © Stockyimages/stock.adobe.com; **p.75** © Rogers Fund, 1917/Metropolitan Museum of Arts; **p.78** © World History Archive/Alamy Stock Photo; **p.79** *br* © Fine Art Images/Heritage Image Partnership Ltd/Alamy Stock Photo, *tc* © INTERFOTO/Alamy Stock Photo, *tl* © INTERFOTO/Alamy Stock Photo, *r* © PAINTING/Alamy Stock Photo; **p.80** © Arsdigital/stock.adobe.com; **p.81** © Paul Fearn/Alamy Stock Photo; **p.82** © Photo Researchers/Science History Images/Alamy Stock Photo; **p.83** *l* © Ivy Close Images/Alamy Stock Photo, *r* © The Granger Collection/Alamy Stock Photo; **p.85** *l* © Classic Image/Alamy Stock Photo, *r* © Fine Art Images/Heritage Image Partnership Ltd/Alamy Stock Photo; **p.86** © Collection/Active Museum/Le Pictorium/ACTIVE MUSEUM/Alamy Stock Photo; **p.87** *t* © Everett Collection Inc/Alamy Stock Photo, *b* © North Wind Picture Archives/Alamy Stock Photo; **p.89** © INTERFOTO/Alamy Stock Photo, © Lebrecht Music and Arts Photo Library/Alamy Stock Photo, © The Artchives/Alamy Stock Photo, © Lebrecht Music and Arts Photo Library/Alamy Stock Photo, © Art Collection 2/Alamy Stock Photo; **p.90** *t* © Lipnitzki/Roger Viollet/Getty Images, *b* © Marco Destefanis/Alamy Stock Photo; **p.93** *l* © Chronicle/Alamy Stock Photo, *r* © Pictorial Press Ltd/Alamy Stock Photo; **p.94** *l* © The Granger Collection / Alamy Stock Photo, *r* © Steve Vidler/Alamy Stock Photo; **p.95** *tl* © Classic Image/Alamy Stock Photo, *bl* © Classic Image/Alamy Stock Photo, *br* © INTERFOTO/Alamy Stock Photo; **p.96** *tc* © Austrian National Library/Interfoto/Alamy Stock Photo, *tr* © Harris Brisbane Dick Fund, 1953/The Metropolitan Museum of Art, *br* © Granger Historical Picture Archive/Alamy Stock Photo; **p.98** © The Print Collector/Heritage Image Partnership Ltd/Alamy Stock Photo; **p.99** © John Hammond/The National Trust Photolibrary/Alamy Stock Photo; **p.102** *t* © Everett Collection Inc/Alamy Stock Photo, *m* © JackF/stock.adobe.com; **p.104** © Pictorial Press Ltd/Alamy Stock Photo; **p.105** Special Collections & College Archives, Musselman Library, Gettysburg College; **p.107** *tr* © World History Archive/Alamy Stock Photo, *br* © Artepics/Alamy Stock Photo; **p.110** © Paul Fearn/Alamy Stock Photo; **p.111** *tc* © Shawshots/Alamy Stock Photo, *tc* © Eddie Gerald/Alamy Stock Photo, *br* © INTERFOTO/Alamy Stock Photo, *bl* © World History Archive/Alamy Stock Photo, *br* © Prisma/Schultz Reinhard/Dukas Presseagentur GmbH/Alamy Stock Photo; **p.112** © Berliner Verlag/Archiv/dpa picture alliance/Alamy Stock Photo; **p.113** © Lebrecht Music and Arts Photo Library/Alamy Stock Photo; **p.118** © YakobchukOlena/stock.adobe.com; **p.120** MANDEL NGAN/AFP/Getty Images; **p.121** *t* © Quint & Lox/Artokoloro Quint Lox Limited/Alamy Stock Photo, *b* © Paul Fearn/Alamy Stock Photo; **p.122** © Georgios Kollidas/Alamy Stock Photo; **p.125** © Granger Historical Picture Archive/Alamy Stock Photo; **p.128** *tl* © Jack Mitchell/Archive Photos/Getty Images, *tc* © Featureflash Photo Agency/Shutterstock.com, *tr* © Fine Art Images/Heritage Image Partnership Ltd/Alamy Stock Photo, *bl* © Robert Nickelsberg/Getty Images, *br* © Bettmann/Getty Images; **p.129** *l* © Ed Emshwiller/Alamy Stock Photo; **p.131** *tr* © Kathryn Kolb, *mr* © Dan Tuffs/Getty Images; **p.132** © Dpa picture alliance/Alamy Stock Photo; **p.133** © Jeff Morgan 03/Alamy Stock Photo; **p.143** *l* © Scott Houston/Alamy Stock Photo, *r* © Margaret Atwood, 02/11/2009, The Handmaid's Tale, Bloomsbury Publishing Plc; **p.147** © Artepics/Alamy Stock Photo.

Text credits

p.6 *t* From City of Ghosts by Bali Rai published by Doubleday Childrens. Reproduced by permission of The Random House Group Ltd., *b* The Scarlet Letter by Nathaniel Hawthorne; **p.8** 'Tanya Landman's top tips for writing historical fiction', theguardian.com © Guardian News & Media Limited; **pp.12–3** Reproduced with permission from Museum of London; **p.14** William Blake, *Holy Thursday*; **p.35** Barkhad Abdi biography. Reprinted with permission of Silver, Massetti & Szatmary Ltd; **p.36** *Life of Johnson*, James Boswell 1791; **p.37** *t* © Lilian Pizzichini, 2009, *The Blue Hour: A Life of Jean Rhys*, Bloomsbury Publishing Plc/W. W. Norton & Company; *c John Lennon: The Life*, Phillip Norman 2008, *b Cristiano Ronaldo: The Biography* Guillem Balague, 2016, © The Orion Publishing Group, London; **p.42** Step back in time, Reproduced with permission of Curtis Brown Group Ltd, on behalf of Antonia Fraser copyright © 2008 Antonia Fraser; **p.45** THEY SAY by Wightman Davidson (2008) 529w from pp.65-66. By permission of Oxford University Press, USA; **p.49** *The Collected Dorothy Parker*, Penguin Books UK; **p.51** *t* From *Jane Eyre, Norton Critical Edition*, Fourth Edition by Charlotte Brontë, edited by Deborah Lutz. Copyright © 2016, 2001, 2000, 1987, 1971 by W.W. Norton & Company, Inc. Used by permission of W. W. Norton & Company, Inc., *b* 'I, Too' from *The Collected Poems of Langston Hughes* by Langston Hughes, edited by Arnold Rampersad with David Roessel, Associate Editor, copyright © 1994 by the Estate of Langston Hughes. Used by permission of David Higham Associates and Alfred A. Knopf, an imprint of the Knopf Doubleday Publishing Group, a division of Penguin Random House LLC. All rights reserved; **p.52** Copyright © Bapsi Sidhwa 1991, published by Daunt Books, 2016; **p.53** From *Alfred Hitchcock* by Peter Ackroyd published by Chatto & Windus. Reprinted by permission of The Random House Group Limited. © 2015 and by permission of Sheil Land Associates on behalf of Peter Ackroyd. **p.61** Introduction to guide to New Zealand by C. N. Baeyertz, 1902; **p.65 and p.75** Extract from Wild Pork and Watercress. Reprinted with permission of Barry Crump estate and Penguin Random House New Zealand; **p.69** *The Canary*, Katherine Mansfield, 1922, Victoria University of Wellington; **p.74** *A Poison Tree*, William Blake; **p.87** *Of Caniballes* by Michel de Montaigne; **p.88** Trinculo in *The Tempest*, Wadsworth Publishing Co Inc; **p.105 and p.116** Letter from *Address Unknown* by Kathrine Kressmann Taylor, © Taylor-Wright Corporation; **p.110** Letter from Cezanne to Emile Zola, J. Paul Getty Museum; **p.113** *l* Quote from *Oliver Twist* by Charles Dickens, *r* Extract from *The Eustace Diamonds*, Anthony Trollope; **p.123** Chapter 1 of *Pride and Prejudice* by Jane Austen, The Republic of Pemberley; **p.125** Extract from *A Room of One's Own* by Virginia Woolf, Penguin Books UK; **p.131** *t Dragonworld* by Zhang Xinxin, translated by Helen Wang, *b The Dispossessed* by Ursula Le Guin, © The Orion Publishing Group, London, and Reprinted with permission of HarperCollins Publishers/AP Watt; **p.132** Copyright © 1979 by Doris Lessing. Featured by kind permission of Jonathan Clowes Ltd., London, on behalf of The Estate of Doris Lessing. Used by permission of Alfred A. Knopf, an imprint of the Knopf Doubleday Publishing Group, a division of Penguin Random House LLC. All rights reserved. **p.134** *Apollo* by Chimamanda Ngozi Adichie. Reprinted with permission of The Wylie Agency; **p.143** From *The Handmaid's Tale* by Margaret Atwood published by Jonathan Cape. Reprinted by permission of The Random House Group Limited. © 1986. Reprinted with permission of Houghton Mifflin Harcourt Publishing Company. All rights reserved. **p.145** Aaj Aakhan Waris Shah Nu by Amrita Pritam, Vikas Publishers; **p.146** *In the Glass Coffin* by Kim Myeong-sun, Reprinted with permisison of Sean Jido Ahn, Translator, *To a Wreath of Snow* by Emily Jane Bronte, Penguin Books; **p.147** *Sweet Torture* by Alfonsia Storni.

t = top, *b* = bottom, *c* = centre, *l* = left, *r* = right